IN THE MYSTERY'S SHADOW

In the Mystery's Shadow

*Reflections on Caring for
the Elderly and Dying*

Susan H. Swetnam

LITURGICAL PRESS
Collegeville, Minnesota

www.litpress.org

© 2019 by Susan H. Swetnam
Published by Liturgical Press, Collegeville, Minnesota. All rights reserved. No part of this book may be used or reproduced in any manner whatsoever, except brief quotations in reviews, without written permission of Liturgical Press, Saint John's Abbey, PO Box 7500, Collegeville, MN 56321-7500. Printed in the United States of America.

1   2   3   4   5   6   7   8   9

Library of Congress Cataloging-in-Publication Data

Names: Swetnam, Susan H., author.
Title: In the mystery's shadow : reflections on caring for the elderly and
    dying / Susan H. Swetnam.
Description: Collegeville : Liturgical Press, 2019.
Identifiers: LCCN 2018050953 (print) | LCCN 2019014582 (ebook) |
    ISBN 9780814663868 (eBook) | ISBN 9780814663622 (pbk.)
Subjects: LCSH: Church work with the terminally ill—Catholic
    Church. | Church work with older people—Catholic Church.
Classification: LCC BV4460.6 (ebook) | LCC BV4460.6 .S94 2019
    (print) | DDC 259/.4—dc23
LC record available at https://lccn.loc.gov/2018050953

To Dr. LaVonne Mills,
to the staff at Heritage Health Services, and
to those whom I've served as a hospice massage therapist,
especially Wanda, Betty, Ina, Geri, Jack, Ned, and Natalie.

Contents

Introduction

Each period of life has its own purpose," writes Joan Chittister in *The Gift of Years: Growing Older Grace-fully*. "The task of [the later years of life] . . . is not simply to endure the coming of the end of time. It is to come alive in ways that I have never been alive before."[1]

A conviction that my own life should "come alive" in new directions led me to a bedside one November afternoon in 2014. Seeking a sense of fresh purpose and daring to imagine that I felt a new calling, I'd retired eighteen months previously from thirty-five years as a university English professor and trained for a second-act career as a massage therapist, hoping to serve not only "regular" clients seeking relief from muscular pain and tension but also the elderly and the dying. After I'd received my new Idaho state massage license (at age sixty-three), a geriatrician much respected in our community had invited me to work as an independent contractor with her clients, and I'd shivered at the apparent evidence of vocation confirmed.

That autumn afternoon on the third day in her employ, however, I felt not happy fruition but panicked doubt. The woman on the bed—nearly a hundred years old but at least fifteen pounds short of that benchmark in weight—stared with bright, mad, darting eyes. Her cheek bones protruded through sunken flesh. Her skin was yellowed, veined, transparent. Her white hair spiked at random angles. Now and then she muttered incomprehensible words; often she whimpered.

I'd seen women like her on the streets of big cities, but she was not homeless. For the past year (and whatever might be left of her future) she'd come to rest in a stark nursing home room whose tightly closed blinds shut out a bright winter day. The walls held photocopied photographs Scotch-taped in place. They depicted long ago family gatherings, images of a much younger woman heartrending in her resemblance to this one, a baby in the arms of a man I knew to be the woman's now-deceased son. A vase of plastic roses perched on a table next to a tiny tube television; a teddy bear lay face down in a corner.

More cheerfully, a pink rose print dotted my patient's rumpled nightgown, perhaps registering that she'd once had a girly streak. The kindly Presbyterian ladies had donated a Project Linus sewing bee blanket adorned with perky pastel kitty cat faces in pansy shapes. Someone had painted eyebrows on the woman's face, but the effect was garish and surreal, suggesting a nightmare Betty Grable after weeks of scavenging in a bombed-out 1946 German city.

I caught a glimpse of myself in a little oval wall mirror, bending over that fragile and uneasy form in a space that smelled more than faintly of urine, gently kneading the impossibly cramped muscles around her shoulder blades, softly circling the tips of my fingers along her bent neck, attempting to warm her hands between mine. *What in the world are you doing here? What made you believe you could comfort the dying?*

Perhaps the noises meant that the woman disliked my touch; conceivably my very presence was making her uneasy. Or maybe the touch wasn't registering at all. Perhaps there was nobody home in an essential human sense in this body, despite the twitches and noises.

I began contriving excuses to flee. If any one of those imaginings was true, surely this session might be cut short. The geriatrician wouldn't want me to continue treatment uncomfortable for the recipient. Another woman in another bed waited a mile away for the next appointment. Perhaps she'd be more responsive.

I'd talked myself into an escape, lifted my touch from the woman's shoulders, and started to straighten when her fingers darted from under the blanket to clutch and squeeze my wrist. She turned toward me, and with great effort her eyes stabilized on mine.

"God bless your hands, dear," she said with perfect clarity, and smiled.

With ten-thousand baby boomers turning sixty-five every day and eighteen percent of the population projected to be over sixty-five by 2030, providing care for the elderly has become an urgent concern in America.[2] According to *US News and World Report*, on any given day in 2016 1.4 million people resided in nursing homes, the vast majority of them elderly.[3] The hospice movement—a multidisciplinary palliative care initiative pioneered in its modern form by Dame Cicely Saunders in London just after World War II—has expanded exponentially.[4] As of 2008, 900,000 people each year were enrolled in hospice care in the United States, including more than a third of dying people.[5]

End-of-life care is in fact already a major occupation, whether unpaid or paid. A 2015 AARP study identified thirty-four million family caregivers in America (people whom the Centers for Disease Control calls "informal" caregivers, a term that will seem misleading to those who discover that such labor consumes their lives).[6] Millions of professionals work in elder care: geriatricians, RNs and LPNs, CNAs, psychologists, social workers, physical and occupational therapists, chaplains, and others (including my own comparatively rare breed, hospice massage therapists). More than 400,000 volunteers supplement family and professional caregivers' work in the United States.[7]

I've been both an "informal" and a professional end-of-life caregiver. My initiation into the realm of palliative care came in 2001–2002 as I tended my husband, Ford, who was dying in his late fifties of prostate cancer—the experience that inspired me to become a hospice massage therapist and ultimately led to this book. As the following pages will describe in more detail, during the last months of Ford's illness a nurse who was also a kind neighbor provided Therapeutic Touch massage (a modality in which the practitioner's hands send healing energy to areas of pain). Though skeptical at the outset I saw how it eased my husband's pain and discovered to my amazement that I was capable of offering such comfort with my own hands.

In the first months of widowhood massage again demonstrated its power after my back froze from the physical pathology of grief. Jolts of debilitating electric pain, apparently random in their onset, coursed from my hip down my leg and up my back. To bend forward, even a little, courted becoming stuck in that position. Running and mountain hiking, habitual go-to tension relaxers, became impossible. Medication, physical therapy, acupuncture and acupressure, chiropractic treatments, psychotherapy, and yoga proved ineffective. Only massage helped me regain the flexibility that made moving around the world in a viable way possible. I now recognize what ailed me as classic piriformis syndrome, but back then it seemed a curse, a punishment, and its abatement at the therapist's hands became a life-changer in more ways than one.

As the spasms and jolts and frozen posture eased and then disappeared I turned back to work, avocations, and friends, slowly settling into a revised way of being that eventually felt like home. Even in the most comfortable of the new normal years, however, I never forgot how touch had helped in the darkest time. An idea began to whisper around the edges of consciousness: when it was time to retire I might make some good from the experience of Ford's death by offering the relief of compassionate touch to other sufferers.

To lay healing hands on strangers in the state of Idaho (and in most others, thank heavens) one has to be certified through education and testing, but the path to that end was fortuitously made straight. The university that employed me offers a massage therapy certificate program in its College of Technology, and I began tentatively, taking career exploration and prerequisite classes during the twilight years of my first-act career, amusing myself and my friends by simultaneously inhabiting roles as University Director of Composition/Unclassified Vo-Tech Student. The fall semester after retirement I began a year of full-time clinical study, followed by a summer internship. So quickly, it seemed, I found myself the sole owner and proprietor of a new one-woman S-Corp, Balsamroot Massage, transformed from a senior full professor in the humanities to an entrepreneur in a minor (some would say marginal) healthcare discipline.

On the whole this second-act career has proven a very good fit. At this writing I've provided thousands of massages, both therapeutic sessions for regular clients in my studio and outcall hospice appointments as an independent contractor. Currently I do at least fifteen massages every week and have offered as many as thirty-six in five days.

While everything about this transformation from knowledge worker to manual laborer still seems unlikely to many who knew me in my previous incarnation, it is the hospice component that inspires the most puzzled remarks.

"Isn't it horribly depressing to work with people who are so sick and so weak?" people ask me. "Why would you want to do that when you retired?"

I always resist what seems to me now an obvious answer—*why wouldn't you want to do that?*—and make some general reply about the satisfaction of comforting vulnerable people. Yet four years on I truly do have trouble imagining how someone could *not* find this work absolutely compelling. Yes, it's physically, psychologically, emotionally, and spiritually taxing, pushing the caregiver to offer more than she could imagine and tempting her to offer more than she *can* give without injury to herself. Serving the elderly and the dying can wear down even the most dedicated in burn-out, causing a practitioner to glide numbly from task to task. Exhaustion can trigger irritability and impatience with the very people whose suffering one seeks to abate and/or with fellow workers, and such responses can inspire recurring doubt about one's own capacity to love, one's own essential worthiness.

I've certainly experienced my share of all of the above. I've also learned, though, that this work of serving the aged and dying offers numerous and varied rewards. Central among them is the altruistic satisfaction of making a difference for someone else. Also compelling is the joy of evolving craft, and the reassurance that one is living as one should, productively and being of service to others.

Less obviously, perhaps, this occupation also offers grati-fications of a more philosophical kind. People doing other kinds of work may be able to ignore the oldest questions: What is the purpose of an individual life and the meaning of its particular duration? How can our lives ever matter, given our flawed nature and the awareness of mortality that threatens to blight our days? Those of us who care for the elderly and people approaching death, however, find them perpetually before us.

Thanks to such inevitable gravitas, the work of elder- and hospice care can feel more like a ministry and an invitation to spiritual journey than like a mere job. We work, one might say, in the very shadow of the divine "Mystery"—a term I'm borrowing from Catholic writer Fr. Richard Rohr, founder of the Center for Contemplation and Action, who uses this term for God to acknowledge the ineffable depths of the divine, the holy that cannot be neatly explained by the human mind.[8]

Once upon a time, when "ministry" was defined as the responsibility of those formally ordained for liturgical ser-vice or as catechists, using the term in this context might have raised eyebrows. That changed in the Catholic Church, however, when Vatican II affirmed the laity's obligation to be "true living witnesses to Christ." Work in the everyday sphere that served a holy purpose was acknowledged as a realm in which the faithful were called to be "light to the world."[9]

While it is inappropriate for those of us employed in secular healthcare contexts to evangelize for particular creeds, we can still be that light, testifying by actions rather than words to the spirit of what we believe. When we do not shrink from the ravages of disease, we affirm that the decline of the physical body does not diminish essential, in-nate human dignity, that the soul is always a glowing thing.

When we serve people suffering from dementia, the handicapped, and the aged with attention and respect, we give the lie to cultural devaluation of people who have "outlived their usefulness" and fold them back into community. When we pick ourselves up and begin again after moments of stumbling, we affirm our acceptance of a grace that reaches to all people despite their imperfections. As we show those we serve by our calm presence that we do not fear death, we demonstrate our abiding hope in eternal life, our trust in what we cannot see.

Most centrally of all, as we caregivers embody love in tending to those who need it most we implicitly witness with our lives that love is inherent in the way humans have been made. We affirm that love is the very essence of the power that created us and guides us always, even when we feel abandoned, even when we do not think about its presence.

"Let all the brothers preach by their works," wrote St. Francis of Assisi on the power of example,[10] a sentiment that might serve as a motto for caregivers.

This book invites those who care for the elderly and the dying (and those considering taking up such work) to view such work through the lens of ministry. It begins with two chapters that establish contexts fundamental to what follows. The first considers end-of-life care from the perspective of vocation in the spiritual sense, reviewing the implications of that term and tracing the various trajectories that such a calling can take. Chapter 2 reviews current attitudes toward aging and dying and argues for a more healthy paradigm, one that affirms the dignity of those nearing the end of life and suggests that they might embrace their later years as an opening rather than as a constriction.

The book's second part, "Practice," consists of eight chapters, each of which considers some particular aspect of elder- and end-of-life service common to caregivers be they family members, volunteers, or professionals. All eight include narrative examples; information from published sources including research-based reports and experts' and spiritual leaders' thinking; and my reflections, which are intended to spark the reader's own meditations rather than being anything like last words on the subject. Topics include the importance of small gestures, the challenge of communicating when patients' cognitive faculties decline, incongruous moments of humor, guilt and burnout, patients who are difficult or who inexplicably seem like soul mates, and uncanny situations where the mystery seems particularly close. The book's final chapter considers that central question voiced early in this introduction: how those of us in end-of-life care can persist in peace and hope in work that reminds us always of human mortality.

The stories and examples recounted are all true, drawn from my experiences and the experiences of the many caregivers interviewed for this book, to whom I offer deep gratitude. Names have been changed and details altered in all cases to protect privacy. While I'm giving acknowledgments, I must also thank Barry Hudock, formerly of Liturgical Press, who encouraged me to write this book and whose faith in my abilities as a writer have sustained me through to its completion.

Obviously this is not a practical how-to book that provides detailed instructions for sickroom techniques or practitioners' self-care; many such resources already exist, some of which are referenced in the pages that follow. Nevertheless,

I hope that both those new to this calling and those who are seasoned professionals will find things in its pages that support their efforts practically, emotionally, and spiritually. In addition, I hope that people who have not previously considered caring for the elderly and the dying, or those who have just begun to imagine doing so, might be inspired by these words to entertain the possibility more seriously.

"Yours is a holy calling," the US Conference of Catholic Bishops advised caregivers, reassuring them that the God who has drawn them to that vocation is always watching over them.[11] Such is the premise of the pages that follow.

PART 1
CONTEXTS

CHAPTER 1

Saying Yes to a Vocation in End-of-Life Care

Ask a professional caregiver who works with the elderly or dying about how he or she got into the business, and you're apt to hear a story about destiny. "I just always knew this was what I should be doing," a young hospice nurse told me, recounting how as a girl she accompanied her grandmother (a woman locally famous as a healer and comforter) when the calls came. "She wasn't formally trained," Lani explained. "But everybody in the little town where I grew up knew her, and everybody in the countryside around." When Lani was eight her grandmother had sensed that she held a gift and made her an apprentice; the little girl spent many nights at bedsides observing, then helping as she grew older. "I loved being a part of that, learning from her," Lani remembered. "I've never wanted to do anything else."

A similar story came from Sarah, a long-time nursing home administrator. "I never thought to wonder why I wanted to follow my mother around when I was little," she said, smiling at the memories. "It just seemed part of who I was. Like taking care of older people was in our genes, or something."

"I've always loved talking to older people," a hospice volunteer proclaimed.

"I've never been afraid to be around people who were dying, and that's why I specialized in geriatrics," a social worker said.

"Because I can," another nurse told me. "That's what I say when people ask why I work with people who are close to passing." The "can" in that sentence, she emphasized, didn't refer only to the skills she'd learned in formal training, essential as they were, but to some capacity for empathy that seemed, well, inborn. When she initially entered nursing school, she briefly thought that she wanted to specialize in sports medicine ("it seemed so glamorous to me at that age, and our trainer had helped me so much when I was in high school sports"). On the first day of geriatric care practicum, however, she instantly felt a clear sense of being in the right place. Though other students teased her "about being Morticia" that sense of inevitable mission didn't go away. "This is what I'm supposed to be doing," she told me. "I was given this capacity for a reason."

As this book begins I think it's important to come clean and emphasize that my origin story regarding this vocation is distinctly different from all of these, not a tale of inborn inclination but an account of a come-lately and on the surface highly unlikely metamorphosis.

In youth and middle age I worked by disposition and choice as a university professor guiding young adults, people on the verge of life rather than nearing its end. I had no idea during my first six decades of how to talk naturally to elderly people. I was phobic about both illness and hospitals. I certainly didn't spend time thinking about my own decline and death or anybody else's. Probably someday, I believe I would have granted (though I don't remember any such perusal), such things would have to be coped with, but that was a bridge to be crossed only when one was forced to come to it.

All I can say is that the Mystery certainly seems to have a sense of humor.

The term "vocation" has come in everyday terminology to mean something like an employment or occupation to which a person is drawn to because it feels very suitable. In the language of faith that "suitable" takes on a weighty and precise implication: a vocation is a divine calling to a particular kind of service. Each of us is endowed with the talents and disposition to serve in a particular way, formed to advance God's agenda. The apostle Paul famously uses the metaphor of the human body to express this concept. As the body consists of many parts with different functions, Paul explains, so too are we each fitted for a specific contribution. "Since we have gifts that differ according to the grace given to us," he writes, "let us exercise them: if prophecy, in proportion to the faith; if ministry, in ministering; if one is a teacher, in teaching; if one exhorts, in exhortation; if one contributes, in generosity; if one is over others, with diligence; if one does acts of mercy, with cheerfulness" (Rom 12:6-8).

"Each one of us has some kind of vocation," Thomas Merton affirms in more modern terms in *No Man Is an Island*. "There is only one thing necessary: to fulfill our own destiny, according to God's will, to be what God wants us to be." Discerning vocation, Merton suggests, is necessarily a co-creative process. The divine provides the gifts and the calling, and, "perfectly confident of being loved by God, the soul that loves Him dares to make a choice of its own, knowing that its choice will be acceptable to love."[1]

As a young person such words would have struck a chord with me, for I definitely felt the pull of vocation . . . though not a vocation in geriatric healthcare. My destiny was words. Writing and making a life as a teacher of writing and literature had appeared from childhood as much of an imperative for me as becoming a hospice nurse had for Lani. I don't remember learning to read; I just could. At age three I incurred my mother's disapproval by filling in an hour every page of a jumbo drawing tablet she'd assumed would occupy me for days, adorning the pages with looping swirls as I pretended to write. I was that uber-serious little girl who always had her head in a book that was supposed to be too advanced for her. A major highlight of my childhood was discovering my father's college literature text (the classic Louis Untermeyer *Modern American Poetry*) tucked in the family bookshelves. The volume became my constant companion, and I still know many of the poems it contains by heart.

Going to college as an English major felt like waking up to who I was supposed to be. After I ran out of graduate degrees to earn I settled down to make a career at a state university in Idaho and married a man who worked beside me, a poet and Wordsworth scholar. Every aspect of the work delighted me. I published articles and books not from obligation but because doing that felt as natural, as inevitable as breathing. I found pleasure in running programs and chairing committees, strange as that might seem. I happily taught general education students, English majors, masters and doctoral students; I taught teachers how to teach. I taught out-of-school adults, too, participating in so many literature and history continuing education programs in far-flung Idaho communities that the state humanities council started calling me its "Road Scholar."

For more than three decades such was my occupation, and it prospered. *I'm exactly where I'm meant to be*, I thought often during that period, feeling the sense of rightness with a palpable warmth.

Then in 1999, twenty years into that career and fourteen into our marriage, my vital husband—flourishing himself as a teacher, writer, and public humanities scholar—was diagnosed with stage four prostate cancer, a rare aggressive viral form that had not made itself known during his PSA the previous year. The idyll dissolved, and at age fifty I found myself "called" to a new role as a family caregiver, an imperative for which nothing had prepared me and that I regarded with utmost apprehension.

At the time the very apprehension itself made me feel guilty, as if I were lacking in some essential feminine (or human) instinct for tending others. Now that I've stepped into hundreds of homes touched by serious illness, however, I've come to understand that most family caregivers share such feelings.

Fortunately for those they serve, many of them overcome initial trepidation and discover in themselves rich resources of resilience, courage, and selflessness. "Oh, I just put one foot in front of the other, one day at a time, and do what has to be done at the moment," one woman remarked when I admired her patience with a mother fretful and demanding with dementia. "What else is there to do? You might as well be cheerful—being hard on her doesn't solve anything." She did apologize for looking tired, explaining that so far that day she'd already cleaned up what sounded like a desperate bathroom mess, soothed a panic attack and spoken on the phone with the doctor about adjusting medication, and called a repairman to address a break in the freezer's icemaker waterline that had sent torrents gushing onto the kitchen floor. The appliances, she remarked, always seem to lie in wait to get you when you're down.

"It is hard when you can't go out even to run errands," the wife caregiver of another of my patients admitted. "At first, I wasn't sure I could take it, being so isolated, so confined to the house. But I love Neil so much, and he's always been so good to me. This is what I'm supposed to do now, to take care of him for better or worse. Well, Parkinson's is certainly worse, but I'm going to do it right." Back in the living room she adjusted her husband's pillows, made sure his water cup was full, and assured him that he should say something if he became uncomfortable, then settled gratefully onto a bench for a caregiver massage. As I soothed her shoulders her husband reached out to touch her hand, beaming up and smiling at me, nodding in obvious delight at this treat for her.

It is one of the great sorrows of my life that I wasn't able to foster such an atmosphere of ease and reassuring comfort for my own husband. Stunned, I pinballed back and forth between anguish and denial, when I might have been manifesting what caregiver manuals call a "healing presence" for him. Luckily for both of us not much actual nursing was required. Since Ford remained outwardly unimpaired and independent my duties consisted largely of being companion, comforter, provider of food, then toward the end house manager and medical liaison. My husband continued teaching at the university during the first of the two years he lived after diagnosis; he drove himself to radiation and chemotherapy. Even as he tired and began spending most of his time in bed he saw a book of poetry through to publication (it won a posthumous prize). He left drafts of new poems composed during his last month of life. Only during the last week of his life was our bedroom an intensive caregiving space, and then professionals came to do the heavy lifting associated with active dying.

As the introduction to this book suggested, however, I did manage to acquire at least one clinical skill when, on a February afternoon in 2002, a neighbor-nurse offered to come to our house and provide Therapeutic Touch, drawing on "healing energy that's around us all the time" to ease my husband's pain. We were dubious, I'll admit—it sounded so new-agey. But she was a highly respected RN, a down-to-earth military reservist and full professor who had helped form generations of nurses at the university. "It can't hurt," Ford said. "Let's see about it."

Within moments it became clear that our neighbor knew what she was about. With quiet concentration she moved confidently to a succession of spots on Ford's back and hip. "That's amazing," he told her. "It doesn't hurt anymore." A serenity descended on the room that calmed even me.

That ease abruptly vanished, though, when she turned in my direction. "Now you try!" she offered with cheerful conviction.

I demurred—I came from a family that did not touch much. I had absolutely no aptitude for this sort of thing.

She insisted, however, and almost at once my hands did indeed sense something, a distinct heat and pulsation on Ford's thigh. The only glitch was that he'd never reported any pain there. Tears of impotency and shame blurred my eyes. "I'm not going to be any good at this," I apologized. "This spot feels funny, angry, but it's not right. It's a false positive. I'm so sorry."

The wonder and sadness in Ford's gaze brought me up short. "Actually, Susan," he said, "I *have* been hurting there a lot recently. I didn't say anything because I didn't want to worry you about bone metathesis."

"You see?" Our neighbor gently touched my shoulder, and I shivered with the sense of having been used, enlisted, in the service of something beyond my ken.

I don't know how I managed to miss all the myriad iterations of "Thy will and not mine be done" I must have heard during a lifetime as a Christian, but I obviously did. I turned fifty as a woman who believed that it was up to her to shape her own destiny, that her own fingers had to grip the wheel if things were to get done, that she had to plan and anticipate every moment of every day.

Ford's death, however, forced the lesson of resignation home. For a long time I felt anger and betrayal. Eventually, though, I granted that unless I wanted to spend the rest of my life in fruitless self-absorbed misery I'd have to agree to let the whys go and face a future that seemed emptied-out and blank. All I could do was to trust that the Mystery did indeed have something in mind for me.

I'm not sure I could have made peace with such surrender without the *Magnificat*, a New Testament passage that became a central supporting text in my early widowhood. "Behold, I am the handmaid of the Lord," Mary says to the angel who comes to tell her that she will carry God's son. "May it be done to me according to your word" (Luke 1:38). In popular parlance this sentiment becomes "Let go and let God," but I persist in affection for the defenseless sense of having "it done to" you, for that's how the whole thing felt as I took the initial steps on that frightening path to whatever came next.

Something changed in me with that setting-out. While I never questioned continued academic vocation—indeed, the faces of students in classrooms and the flow of words on pages went a long way toward enabling me to continue after Ford's death—I began to feel different, set apart from rationalist colleagues who so firmly believed in their own agency. The self-determined can-do "little guided missile" (as Ford had affectionately called me) had vanished. The woman who stood in her place began to learn to make her peace (mostly) with things she could not control, to ask, "Okay, what's next?" with trust. She learned that "hunches" and "accidents" could lead to the most perfect, life-giving moments.

My affect become more vulnerable, softer. As a university professor I'd never been one to draw the sisters of tragedy, those students who bring to office hours tales of personal suffering and beg for counselor-style advice, support, redemptive inspiration. After I was widowed, though, they flocked to me, the undergrads confessing to unwanted pregnancy, spousal and/or drug abuse, depression; the graduate students agonizing over crises in teaching vocation. A suicidal young poet came in tears one afternoon. "Help me," she begged. "Teach me what you've learned about how to live." I began to imagine myself as a soul-sister to Nathaniel Hawthorne's Hester Prynne in *The Scarlet Letter*, a woman wearing a visible sign of her suffering. Mine was not a literal "A" inscribed on my dress but a less tangible "G" for "grief" inscribed in my spirit, an emanation that seemed to beckon to those struggling with their own private pain. Though I'd always considered myself brisk and impatient, it was now easy to sit quietly in empathy, asking, listening, counseling.

Despite such experiences I entered massage therapy training inwardly dubious about my aptitude for ministering to strangers—especially uncongenial strangers—and continued to question well into the first semester. The night that changed my mind finally arrived four months along, on a November night in student clinic when I drew a self-described "like totally stressed out" young undergraduate woman, one of those pert, disorganized, cliché-ridden, apparently silly girls who had always driven me crazy when they appeared in my classrooms, the ones who habitually asked "will this be on the test?" and "are we going to do anything in class today?" *Oh boy*, I thought as she took forever to settle on the table, fidgeting with superfluous energy. *How are you going to be able to calm somebody who's making YOU so nervous?*

To my surprise the young woman went to sleep a few minutes into the massage, and I felt suddenly wrapped in compassion, breathing it through my hands as I worked, wishing her peace.

As darkness fell I gazed out the classroom window at the year's first snowfall drifting down through the lights of a four-story dormitory across the way. I imagined the other young people behind those windows worrying about their classes, their capacities as students, whether or not anybody would ever love them. I thought of them struggling with decisions about short- and long-term paths, about failures, about what would "be on the test." My heart opened of its own accord, and I spontaneously breathed peace to them too, and even greater comfort to the girl on the table. With a rush of quiet joy my own mind and body relaxed as the certainty came: *This is going to be all right. You can do this.*

And that was how the Mystery nudged/guided/dragooned this life-long head-worker into becoming a hand (and heart, and soul) worker.

If you're a reader of contemporary self-help literature you'll probably have encountered the contention that embracing vocation (also known as "following your passion") will inevitably lead to happiness and success. "Three Signs You Are Following Your Passion: 1. Joy, 2. Love, 3. Ease" proclaims a meme along this line that one of my Facebook friends shared recently.

If only it were so easy, so consistent. Naturally if what you're doing always makes you miserable it's probably a sign that you're in the wrong business, but in reality practicing even a true vocation can be hard, discouraging work. This isn't new news: both the Old and the New Testaments are full of examples of people who are mortally unhappy about the paths to which God has called them and/or the twists and turns that those paths take. Moses protests to God, "Who am I that I should go to Pharaoh and lead the Israelites out of Egypt?" He gripes about the recalcitrance of said Israelites during the pilgrimage to the promised land ("What shall I do with these people?" he cries when they demand that he give them nonexistent water) (Exod 3:11; 17:4). Jonah attempts to run away from the obligation to preach at Nineveh (look where that gets him). Prophets and apostles are reviled and/or killed while doing what God has called them to do. Jesus himself expresses anguish on the cross ("My God, my God, why have you forsaken me?") (Mark 15:34).

Stories told about Catholic saints reveal that some also struggled with their callings. St. John Vianney is said to have become so exhausted that he tried to flee the thousands who came to him for confession. St. Frances Xavier Cabrini insisted repeatedly to her superior (though in vain) that she was meant to be a missionary in China instead of in the United States. Elizabeth Seton (my patron, a widow and educator) suffered depression even after she'd succeeded, against great odds, in establishing the first (and flourishing) Catholic girls' school in America. "Here I go," she wrote in a letter to a friend during a period when friends and relatives were dying and she was exhausted, "like iron or rock, day after day, as [God] pleases and how he pleases; but to be sure, when my time comes, I shall be very glad."[2]

I find such stories comforting because, frankly, they reflect my own admittedly as-yet imperfect acquiescence. You're not required always to like the hand that God has dealt you, they suggest. You're not failing if you can't adopt a perfectly ego-free, angelically smiling prostration. What you are asked to do is simply to persist in faith even when that faith makes no sense to human intellect.

As generations of wise ones have emphasized, cultivating such surrender—perfect or not as it may be in any given moment—is good for us in many senses. It fosters dependence on God. "You have understood who is the Artisan, do not be curious as to how; you have understood who is the sculptor, do not ask questions about the work," proclaims a fourth-century homily on the Annunciation by Pseudo-Chrysostom.[3] "We must put all speculation aside and, with childlike willingness, accept all that God presents to us," writes early eighteenth-century French Jesuit Jean-Pierre de Caussade.[4]

Taking Mary as a model can also help free us from the trap of self-absorption, a lesson I learned on my own the hard way, as noted above. Contemporary Jungian psychologist David Richo explains that when the Virgin proclaims, "Let it be done to thee according to Thy will" at the annunciation, she demonstrates that humans can transcend selfish ego and embrace a higher self that is aligned with the divine. "In mature spirituality," he writes, "we do not pray for the conditions of existence to be different but for the grace to say yes to them without protest or blame of God or humanity . . . when control disappears, God appears."[5] Once we move beyond ego into grace, we are free to find the purpose for which we were born. "The vocation of each one of us," Thomas Merton writes, "is fixed just as much by the need others have for us as by our own need for other[s] . . . and for God." Saying yes to a particular calling represents "an act that gathers up all the powers and capacities of our being" and offers them in trust to the divine will.[6]

Early in my massage career a woman who has since moved to another state came to my studio seeking weekly massages for what she termed "regular maintenance and pampering." To all appearances and in her medical records she appeared quite healthy for her sixty-two years. She reported daily walks, a healthy diet heavy on plants and light on red meat, acceptable bloodwork numbers and weight. She described a "stress-free" life as a retiree whose husband continued to earn a very comfortable living.

Yet she was miserable, prone to unexplained back aches and headaches, her sleep uneasy, her blood pressure tending high. From the first appointment she talked incessantly, compulsively, recounting the plays she and her husband had seen, the concerts they'd attended, her visits to friends in distant cities, their past and upcoming trips to Europe, the extensive redecorations of kitchen, bathrooms, and gardens she'd orchestrated. She spoke endlessly about friends', children's, and grandchildren's accomplishments.

At first such recitals struck me as bragging and put me off, but soon I understood that pity would be a more appropriate response. This woman had no one else to talk to;

she was terribly bored. "Oh, I sleep in late!" she proclaimed. "After all, I'm retired. Just drinking coffee and reading the newspaper can take all morning!" She took walks and puttered while her husband worked, went shopping or sat in the sun reading "fun" books. After dinner (usually takeout or delivery; after a lifetime of cooking, she said, she was tired of that) they watched Netflix.

As our time together extended she grew more confessional, and one afternoon she began to complain about how much her husband worked, how imperious and oblivious to her he could be. "You don't know how it is, to be taken for granted," she said. "You have this business, and people depend on you. But with the kids gone, for me it's just Tom. And so often he seems to be somewhere else, even when he's there. I feel like I'm not real sometimes, like I don't exist."

Had she ever thought of volunteering? Anyone could be trained and serve an hour or two a week visiting hospice patients and the elderly. There was nobody to whom presence mattered more than such people, and if she had time on her hands and wanted to be warmly appreciated, that was the perfect opportunity.

"Oh no, I could never do that." The reply was instant, emphatic. "I'm not that kind of person. I'm sensitive; I couldn't take blood or suffering or being around dying people." So what about volunteering at the library, or tutoring kids in reading at the elementary school near her home, or taking a look, just for fun, at the "volunteers needed" column of the weekly newspaper? No, no, and no. "I worked all my life, and I've earned a rest!"

That week I'd already provided more than twenty massages, with one additional, even-more-crammed workday to go. Thus "I've earned a rest" struck my ears with seductive import. *Why not me, too?*

But after she left a cancer survivor came in for a lymph-edema massage, and then a man who had lost his wife six months earlier, and at the day's end I spent half an hour in a nursing home with a courtly gent in his eighties who ceremonially kissed my hand in greeting and again in farewell.

I drove home at six-thirty smiling at those immediate memories, the hour making me remember that Lani was just beginning her work day, a full night on call for emergencies. I imagined Sarah sitting at the bedside of an occupant of her nursing home, and the wife-caregiver I'd seen earlier that week fixing a loving dinner for her husband with Parkinson's. I anticipated the morrow's round of hospice massages, the smiles at my appearance, the hands reaching to squeeze mine, the contagious peace.

And I allowed myself to imagine, for just a moment, what life might have been like at that moment if Ford had died and I'd come to a retirement that included only relaxation. What unimaginable grace it was to have been granted the courage to say yes, to surrender in trust to this most unlikely vocation. What a gift to have been led, even through suffering and loss, to this blessed, still-evolving path.

CHAPTER 2

Honoring the Rich Possibilities of Aging

The fear of diminished capacity and agency in old age has been a perennial theme in literature, considered in some of our oldest myths and tales. Shakespeare's tragedy *King Lear* is among the narratives that chronicle how even the strongest of the elderly can be demeaned, as Lear's two older daughters employ timeless stereotypes to justify their usurpation of his power and wealth. Her father, says Lear's daughter Goneril, can only be expected to exhibit "the unruly waywardness that infirm and choleric years bring with them." "O, sir, you are old! / . . . . You should be rul'd, and led / By some discretion that discerns your state / Better than you yourself," the King's other custodial daughter, Regan, informs him.

American poet Robert Frost's 1915 "The Oven Bird" voices a poignant melancholy as its narrator anticipates the passage of time. Though the bird depicted in the poem sings in midsummer, Frost imagines that it is already obsessed with the looming and inevitable change of seasons, lamenting the long-past bloom of spring flowers and the aging of leaves that anticipates autumn. Evoking the human life span as well as natural cycles, the poem concludes with an unanswered question. How might one respond and persevere given the inevitable diminution that aging brings? That query remains not only relevant but of urgent importance in the twenty-first century. For, as legions of cultural commentators and sociologists and pop psychologists have proclaimed, in Western culture not only do the elderly have to grapple with the classic questions about how their lives can continue to have meaning, but also with particular contemporary devaluation and disrespect. America is famously a youth-centric society, one that worships young energy and beauty and possibility. Older people are considered unattractive, pathetic, ridiculous. In recent years they have even been castigated for the burden they will allegedly place on the American economy and infrastructure as baby boomers age.[2]

"There is so much shame in our culture around aging and death," writes Koshin Paley Ellison, cofounder of the New York Zen Center for Contemplative Care.[3]

A mega anti-aging industry preys on such attitudes. Celebrities, medical professionals, aspiring entrepreneurs, holistic healers, and quacks tout potions, plastic surgery, Botox injections, and rejuvenation clinics that purport to "attack" and "defeat" physical aging. Even if we do look a little past our prime, life coaches catering to seniors assure us, patented fitness regimes and positive thinking protocols can make age "just a number." Media images foster such fantasies by featuring glamourous outliers: *U.S.A. Today* profiled an 80-year old male marathoner; television advertisements depict beautiful aging couples golfing or skydiving together; even the cover of the *AARP Magazine* (sigh) often features mature models with "sexy at sixty" appeal.

One of the most tragicomically memorable moments in my hospice career involved such peddling of this impossible fantasy. "Would you look at that!" a frail man in a bed exclaimed to me. In the past he'd been confused or silent during my visits, and I turned to the television to see what had inspired that burst of lively cogency. The image was compelling, all right: a woman said to be seventy-five—just five years younger than he—pole dancing in a skin-tight cat suit.

She was not, I hasten to add, on the stage of a strip club (even *Inside Edition* wouldn't go that far) but in a gym, doing gravity-defying moves including horizontal suspension off the pole. She looked great in a dancer's leotard and tights, lean and muscularly defined, her high blonde ponytail bouncing to a hip-hop beat as she instructed much younger students.

"That's really something!" my patient repeated. "She's a real role model for the rest of us. If you started now, I bet you could do that too!" And then, overwrought, he burst into a coughing fit so severe I had to call a nurse. It was like something out of Dickens.

"After watching a summer's worth of daytime TV ads," one of my Facebook friends, a woman in her seventies, posted last August, "I feel like I have a lot of nerve merely existing at my age, like I'm supposed to just crawl off and die."

I hear her, because even though I'm in decent physical shape in my late sixties, still walking, jogging, hiking, or seasonally cross-country skiing multiple times a week, I still can't quite shake the sense of inadequacy, and, yes, of body shame which that "glamorous pole-dancing granny" (as the commentator called her) has inspired in me.

The roots of elder-shame run deeper than mere physical appearance, according to geriatric physician William H. Thomas. Thanks to the historic influences of Calvinism and our capitalist culture, he argues, we've embraced busyness and tangible productivity as totem virtues. We value doing over being and thus embrace a "cult of adulthood" that celebrates the working years as life's zenith. People who have aged to where they can no longer continue to rack up lists of successes are seen as "failed adults," lame ducks living beyond life's purpose.[4]

Such attitudes can have dire consequences for the elderly. Even simply retiring and thus losing the sense of identity that a job provides makes people 40 percent more likely to suffer from depression, according to a 2013 study sponsored by the British Institute of Economic Affairs and Age Endeavor Fellowship. That same study found that retirees are also 60 percent more likely to develop a new serious physical ailment than people their age still employed.[5]

Those who become unable to care for themselves face particular risks related to diminished self-esteem. Rates of depression have been estimated as high as 45 percent for nursing home residents, and late-life depression in particular, Amy Fiske and her colleagues emphasize in a 2009 article in *The Annual Review of Clinical Psychology*, can have terrible objective consequences. Those who suffer from it are likely to experience steeper physical, cognitive, and social decline; are likely to die sooner from natural medical causes; and face higher odds of suicide.[6]

"The battle of being mortal," writes physician and best-selling writer Atul Gawande, "is the battle to maintain the integrity of one's life—to avoid becoming so diminished or dissipated or subjugated that who you are becomes disconnected from who you were or who you want to be." Gawande contends that conventional contemporary strategies for tending the aging, though well-meant, represent a "failed experiment" in promoting such integrity. Long-term care facilities emphasize custodial safety and efficiency of care but drastically, tragically erode residents' ability to live lives of "worth and purpose." Apparently mundane matters such as lack of food choice, standardized bedtimes, and "nannying" prohibition of lifelong habits or tastes for someone's "own good" can become for symbols of loss of autonomy, straws that break the desire to live.[7]

One of my patients was broken in just that way. She'd been recently admitted to a luxurious nursing home when I first met her, but she was already plenty angry. She'd always lived alone and managed her own affairs as a single working woman, she told me with pride as I massaged her feet, and she'd done a very good job. "I'm capable of knowing what I need," she proclaimed. Then the tears and the complaints began to flow. She'd always been a night owl—she loved the night's quiet, could think better then. She only felt good if she stayed up till one or two in the morning and woke at nine. "But here they make me go to bed at eight!" she wailed. "I feel so disoriented! What harm is it doing if I stay up! But even if I get into bed when they say like a good little girl then stay up and read all by myself in bed—not giving any trouble to anybody—they see the light and come in and turn it off and scold me."

What harm, indeed?—but efforts to win a reprieve for her came to naught. The facility brought in staff in the early evening specifically to help with bedtime preparation, I was told with looks that said *troublemaker!* They couldn't have people sleeping on irregular schedules since meals and personal care happened at particular times. And just how was this my business, anyway?

Three months later the night owl gave up and sank into silence; three months after that she was gone.

Even people who prove compliant can find their tenuous dignity eroded by the persistent culture of infantilization in assisted living facilities. Treating the aged as children may be intended as a kind suggestion of love and cossetting, a promise that there is nothing to fear. Yet it's ultimately demeaning. I'm always surprised that others don't wince as I do when residents are spoken to in sing-song baby talk and addressed in the patronizing first person plural as if they were toddlers ("Do we want some of this nice applesauce?"). Familiar nick-names ("diminutives," they're called for a reason) are the standard choice of appellation in several facilities I visit. "He's always been 'Robert,' not 'Bobby,' but that's what they call him here, and I've given up," a patient's wife told me. "All I can do is hope he's okay with that." Dining tables sport elementary-school-style place cards adorned with seasonal stickers; glitter adorns name plates on bedroom doors (pink for girls, blue for boys). Recreational activities are of the kindergarten persuasion, heavy on bingo and other mindless entertainment. I once saw a former university dean coerced to play along with a "fun game" that involved tossing beanbags into a cardboard bear's mouth. I witnessed a man who had managed a multimillion-dollar ranch wheeled down the hall over his protests, forced to join others for a cartoon movie featuring horses "because you LIKE horses."

Scientific studies of the effects of such infantilization (as you might anticipate) reliably confirm that elders find it demeaning and respond with anger or sullen withdrawal. More alarmingly yet, considerable evidence suggests that infantilization can encourage new or more intense symptoms of dementia.[8]

Even in the midst of such bombardment there are those who somehow manage to resist being cast as children, and these rebels have become my new heroes. One of particular

mettle is my patient Beatrice, a former hospital administrator. "I don't want to take that now," she insisted to a young
woman in Mickey Mouse scrubs proffering a tiny paper
cup. "The doctor said I could take them or not, as I wanted.
They're going to make me sleepy right away if I take them
now, and I want to enjoy this massage in my right mind. I
want to talk to Susan."

The aide stiffened. "Oh hon," she wheedled. "O Bea, I
think you should. Come on. Pretty please?"

"NO!" Beatrice leaned forward in her bed with great
emphasis. "Do you hear me? I said, 'No!' Later on, after dinner, fine. Call the doctor if you want to check, but he'll say
what I said. It's up to me. I don't need to be overmedicated."

The aide looked at me, beseeching. I shrugged, panto-
miming helplessness.

She glared—*traitor! You should be on our side!*—sniffed
audibly, and stalked out. "Bea is so stubborn," we heard her
telling someone in the hall, making no effort to lower her
voice. "Her tantrums are driving me crazy!"

"Well," Beatrice offered, a gleam in her eye, "at least I'm
not 'adorable' today, and that's something."

Pope Francis has repeatedly condemned contemporary
disrespect for the elderly. We live in a "throwaway culture"
regarding human life, he chastens, one that denies the value
of the vulnerable and so-called useless members of society,
including the elderly. It's our duty as people of faith, people
who aspire to live principled lives, to turn away from such
destructive attitudes. We must heed scripture, which emphasizes honoring the wisdom of the elderly and instructs
us to care with utmost respect for them. The aging not only

remain children of God possessed of holy souls, but this stage of life in particular constitutes "a time of grace" with its own distinctive "true mission from the Lord" and "true value." Instead of ignoring and discarding the elderly, we must recognize them as called to be "trees that continue to bear much fruit." "We must awaken the collective sense of gratitude, of appreciation, of hospitality, which makes the elder feel like a living part of his community," he proclaimed in a 2015 address.[9]

A 1999 statement on aging by the US Conference of Catholic Bishops anticipated Francis's sentiments, calling on the faithful to "cherish the whole person, with his gifts and talents as well as limitations and vulnerabilities" in old age. Later years offer their own distinctive and marvelous opportunities, the bishops write. With "time and space to reflect more deeply and to act with greater moral grounding and vision" the aged can engage more fully in prayer and contemplation. They have the opportunity to review their lives and extend forgiveness to themselves and others. They're perfectly positioned to celebrate interdependence by cultivating relationships in which they both receive and confer blessings, sharing wisdom with the young and with their communities, and reaching out in service to others. The bishops term the latter "a responsibility, commensurate with health, abilities, and other obligations." Even if homebound and frail the elderly can witness faith to those around them.[10]

In recent years excellent books from a variety of viewpoints and spiritual traditions have brought this old-new paradigm of aging to general readers. William Thomas's *What Are Old People For?* argues that if our culture is to flourish it must draw on elders' wise long view. Lewis Richmond's *Aging As a Spiritual Practice* brings a Buddhist perspective to the topic, explaining that aging can move us toward wisdom as the bonds of our ego loosen, we learn to accept change, and we discover a deeper sense of unity with others.[11] Thomas Moore, a popular spiritual writer and Jungian psychotherapist, invites his readers to imagine life's stages as a series of initiations that lead progressively to greater fulfillment.[12]

Two books by Catholic writers alluded to briefly in previous chapters of this book consider in particular depth how the very changes in physical prowess, brain chemistry, and consequent "productivity" that our culture derides can actually be portals to profound new insight. The inevitable losses of our lives, Fr. Richard Rohr contends in *Falling Upward: A Spirituality for the Two Halves of Life*, challenge the neatly coherent stories we've been telling about ourselves, others, and God through the "productive" ego-driven adult stage of life. The very uncertainty, sadness, and fright such diminishments evoke invite us to soften our boundaries and relax our control, allowing for a more mature spirituality. Sr. Joan Chittister's *The Gift of Years: Growing Older Gracefully* argues that while old age brings burdens, its slower pace invites us to seek our true selves and to cultivate surrender in trust to the embrace of a loving and forgiving God. Chittister emphasizes that this call to contemplation does not absolve the elderly of the call to serve others. "Age does not forgive us our responsibility to give the world back to God a bit better than it was because we were here. . . . The last phase of life is not non-life; it is a *new* stage of life . . . maybe the most special of them all," Chittister insists.[13]

She and Rohr as well as the others writers alluded to above provide suggestions of how such engagement might manifest in action: deepening friendships, community service and social justice work, artistic exploration, study and discussion with others, mentoring. Even if such tangible contributions become impossible, those nearing the end of life can offer prayer and/or the grateful appreciative noticing of the world's gifts that is a sort of prayer. They can reflect on the past and seek reconciliation with self and others. They can manifest to those around them what sacred acceptance of the divine's mysterious ways might look like.

Such thinking stands contemporary age-phobia on its head. Life does not end when our vigor and productivity does, it insists. God-given new birthing always going on, and we should "not [be] discouraged" but rather trust that "although our outer self is wasting away, our inner self is being renewed day by day" (2 Cor 4:16). What we do in the last years of life is every bit as essential to the development of our souls as what we accomplished in our "prime." If we are willing to open and listen to the possibilities of the evolving present, meaning and God-given dignity will continue to be ours all the days of our lives . . . and after, but that's a subject for a later chapter.

It's exciting to encounter people—both caregivers and the elderly—who insist on living out that promise despite our culture's toxic paradigms. Among them is a woman I met who stood up to an assisted living facility's underselling of its residents. After her mother, my patient, moved into the facility, this woman, Sandy, volunteered to lead a chair yoga class but was discouraged from even attempting such an activity. Residents wouldn't be interested in that, she was told. They couldn't manage such "physical" and "taxing" new activities. They much preferred things like listening to those who came to play music for them, ice cream parties, and, well, bingo. "Let's give it a try," Sandy insisted.

So many people now attend that class that it has out-grown the little room to which it was initially assigned. Sessions now take place in the facility's main activity area, where residents can look out on beautiful plantings and natural light as they practice. "We may have to start a second class," Sandy reported. "Even that big room's getting pretty jammed."

Meanwhile her mother—a woman of continued intellectual curiosity and determination though growing frail in her nineties—has despite similar skepticism organized the first-ever book club in that facility. Five women who would otherwise be sitting idle and bored in their rooms now read in preparation and meet every week to share their thoughts. That's not a large number, Sandy's mother admits with a shrug, but they've recently decided to hold sessions in a public space rather than in someone's room so that others will see how much fun they're having. "Reading is so good for older people, don't you think?" she asks. Then, ever the go-getter, she charmingly wheedles: "Do you think you could come and talk to us sometimes about the book we're reading? I bet you miss teaching!"

Among such "soul friends, gurus, confessors, mentors, masters, and spiritual directors" (to borrow a phrase from Rohr)[14] who by example are helping me face my own aging with less fear is one of my patients who found her life gloriously expanded in old age though she endured that period of life under the most inauspicious circumstances.

A heavy-set woman crippled by arthritis and weakened by diabetes and COPD, Clare hadn't finished high school. At age seventy-nine her dwindling savings had forced her from the frame house by the railroad tracks where she and her late husband had raised ten children into one of the only places in town she could afford, a studio apartment in a complex often featured in the police log for drugs, domestic violence, and robbery.

Once an active bustling woman, Clare spent most of her time in a recliner facing a parking lot where all kinds of characters came and went. Only one of her children lived nearby, a gruff man who dropped in to tend her mornings and evenings but spent most of his time in the apartment, at least when I was there, glued to Fox News and police-chase reality shows rather than interacting with his mother.

Yet the Clare who became my friend was cheerful, a woman who had found in the period of limitation a flowering of creativity and service. She was, she informed me when we met, "a born-again needle worker." As a girl back in Arkansas she'd loved to crochet (her grandmother had called her "a natural," a designation of which she was still very proud), but what with raising all those kids and supplementing family income with work as a school lunch lady and an office cleaner . . . well, there just hadn't been much time for handiwork once she got into her twenties. Soon after Clare's move to the studio apartment, however, a woman from her church had come to visit and they'd "gotten to talkin' lady stuff," including needlework. Within days Clare's Mormon bishop appeared at the door with an invitation and a big plastic bin full of yarn, hooks and needles, and patterns. The ward (congregation) she belonged to needed somebody to make items for charity, he informed her, and if she'd accept that responsibility he'd make sure the bin was replenished.

"I was so excited," Clare said. "I'd just been sitting around like a bump on a log for so long, and it was making me feel so down." Now she had much to do in fulfilling all those orders for blankets, mittens, prayer shawls, slippers, and most of all, hats. "I've made more than 500 hats for the homeless!" she proudly informed me. She'd even been blessed to witness with her own eyes the happy consequence of her labor: the past winter her son had taken her out to dinner in a fast-food restaurant downtown and through the window she'd seen destitute person after destitute person passing by wearing a piece from her hands. " 'There goes another one of my hats!' I kept sayin'!" she said gleefully.

In no way did Clare undertake this mission in the spirit of dogged poorhouse obligation; she dug into her assignments with vigorous delight. After someone called her "a fiber artist," she proudly adopted that term for herself. It was in fact not an unreasonable appellation. Though Clare worked mostly with cheap acrylic yarn, she possessed a striking design sense and an inventive spirit. Her eagerness to grow in the craft was obvious in the needlework-nerd topics that dominated our conversations during massages. As a knitter myself, what did I think of this color combination? Which of these edgings would go best with this blanket? Did this open-work pattern (that she was even then inventing) look "right" with that yarn? She demanded that I bring my own completed pieces to show her and admired them with vigor. Toward the end, when her fingers finally cramped enough that crocheting was impossible, I was the one to whom she offered her stash to "share with people in need." I duly gave it to another saint, one who teaches needle arts to at-risk teenagers and people with mental illness.

I still think of Clare when I pass that apartment complex, imagining my friend now in a perfect postcard heaven. I fancy her once-again newly nimble fingers reaching into a new bin, this one filled with yarn worthy of her skills (to my mind if you have to work with acrylic, it's not heaven) and her exclamations at the marvelous textures, the subtle colors. Most of all, I like to picture this friend above sitting on a cloud, exalting, "There goes another one of my hats!" as a slightly scruffy (though warm-headed) angel floats by.

All of the above examples, you may have noticed, involve active adulting-doing-style contribution in old age, and I'll admit that slant says something about me. I remain even in "retirement" an inveterate doer, as this book should make obvious. Though I believe absolutely that elders can live holy and valuable lives just by their presence, I'll admit to apprehension about my capacity to make peace if future limitations call me to a purely "being" life.

This past winter, however, I acquired a mentor in that regard, a patient who came into my life on the exact day when I most needed her uplifting example.

The month was December, the day's circumstances guaranteed to convince anyone that old age necessarily leads to diminishment. All of my massage assignments had taken me to nursing homes that rolled in forced (and crass, and inappropriate) Christmas jollity. I'd given massages to people festooned as they slept in wheelchairs with Santa hats, jingle bells, and foam reindeer antlers. I'd seen a "May Your Days Be Merry and Bright!" banner in a critical care unit. I'd heard playlists heavy on seasonal music for children (The Chipmunks appeared with regularity) and songs breathtakingly tone deaf in their content (one loop included "Grandma Got Run Over by a Reindeer"—I'm not making this up). I'd been present when an activities director burst into a room where a man lay exhausted from hallucinations and invited his wife to "come on down!" to a Christmas root beer float party.

Just shoot me the moment this becomes my reality, I'd caught myself thinking on the drive out into the country to Myra's address, the final massage of the day.

All was calm, though, in the old farm house. "That's our tree this year," the man said, pointing to the Christmas cactus that filled a bay window. The plant was hard to miss, a good three feet in diameter and nearly as high, decades old and flowering enthusiastically in scarlet red, decked with glittering balls and strings of mini-lights glowing against the fading late-afternoon sun.

"We just didn't want to bother with a big tree this year," the frail woman in the headscarf—Myra—chipped in from her armchair. "Besides, it seemed like that plant had earned the honor!"

Her husband laughed, hitching up his overalls. "She's just being nice," he told me. "What she means is that I couldn't handle a tree with this hip."

"It's beautiful," she insisted. "Come on, admit it!"

As I oh-so-gently kneaded her emaciated shoulders, cradled and stretched her bony arms, stroked her hands with their now-slack skin, she beamed at me.

"This is going to be a different kind of Christmas," she told me. "But I'm so excited for it." She admitted that she'd never been the type to want help in the kitchen, reminiscing with evident pride about the feasts she always prepared for holidays past in the tiny galley space visible over her shoulder. This year, though, her adult daughter had volunteered to cook, "and I'm just going to sit like a lazy thing, watching her do all the work and spoiling the grandchildren! You know, I'm looking forward to that. I know she's going to enjoy it, and it's going to be fun to see how she makes Mother's recipes."

Another big change, Myra said, was that they were going to have "different company." Christmas had always been a strictly family time, but her son who worked at the university had made friends with a young couple from Indonesia (he spoke their language because of his Mormon mission) and they'd come to meet Myra, and they'd all gotten along so well, and those kids didn't have any place to go for the holiday. Well, not their holiday, exactly—they were Muslim. But they'd promised to share some seasonal customs of their own. "So we have an even bigger family this year!" She spread her hands in an embrace of infinitely expandable love.

Then she cocked her head and assessed me. "And what about you? You're a widow, you said? Do you have a place to go? There's always room for one more."

I already did have a place to go, though the idea of what Myra's neighbors in this insular community might say if the "different" company included Muslims *and* a strange single woman made me smile.

No one in that house was deceiving themselves about Myra's long odds of ever celebrating another nativity on earth; she'd decided to forego chemotherapy and settled into the future with serene resolve. Nobody had insisted on all the usual Christmas trappings, nor forced merriment.

Yet the season's essential cheer gleamed in the house, palpable as that repurposed cactus. Its message of peace among peoples and hopeful trust in God's promise sparkled in that still and elderly woman. Myra had become a model for everyone around her of the holiest kind of peace, the absolute embodiment of let-it-be faith—an ultimate Christmas gift, though she was a woman who might be judged in the wider world as beyond ever giving anything to anyone again.

When I was a young adult in college literature classes I remember being deeply moved by Dylan Thomas's poem, "Do Not Go Gentle Into That Good Night," with its call to struggle against death right up until the end. The students

I later taught were, too, for discussion always soared when that poem was its subject. Once I had to throw a cluster of students out of the room as they lingered in discussion even as the instructor of the following class wrote notes on the board and her students, glaring, settled around the stragglers.

It's indeed a lovely poem. I've come to believe, however, that it's a young person's poem (Thomas was in his thirties when he wrote it). Raging against old age and death sounds good in theory, especially if your life is just beginning. But when the inevitable changes of aging come, trying to cling to what is gone forever can only lead to misery—and to blindness regarding the rich possibilities implicit in even the last days of a life.

The call of old age, Rohr writes, is "not so much *to have what you love* anymore, but *to love what you have*—right now."[15] All who care for those whose days are growing short would do well to encourage such a sentiment in those we serve, both by witnessing with gladness our embrace of our own "right now" and by encouraging our elderly friends to rise each day anticipating the gifts it might offer . . . or the gifts that they might offer to others.

PART 2
PRACTICE

CHAPTER 3

The Little Things

They're so idealistic," the woman says. This retired RN, my neighbor-nurse's colleague, smiles at memories of the student nurses whom she mentored. "They start their first jobs thinking they're going to save the world. Especially the ones who want to work with vulnerable populations like children, the elderly, people with advanced cancer. They dream of big dramatic moments—they've watched *ER*, after all. They imagine being healers with superhuman powers, wonder-workers who come up with cures that nobody else would imagine."

I nod, remembering a conversation with another RN now employed in geriatric care. "Twenty years ago I thought I was going to perform miracles," she said when interviewed for this book. "With my shiny-new bag of tricks and my love, I imagined all kinds of grand gestures that would have people gasping—I was going to be a legend!"

"But the real nursing comes," the first nurse continues, "as I always tell them, not in the big things you might get to do occasionally but in the little things you do every day. All those unglamorous, unremarkable, simple actions of caring."

Although those who work with the elderly and the dying cannot aspire to cure old age or terminal disease, big things are indubitably among the responsibilities many undertake. Practitioners analyze and manage pain, both acute and chronic. They address anxiety and depression. They must be able to choose appropriately from a range of non-pharmaceutical (cognitive therapy, guided imagery, relaxation, meditation, etc.) and pharmaceutical alternatives. They are required to assess the effectiveness and dosage level of drugs and to manage care appliances. They must monitor vital signs and respond to events that require new interventions. They are called to recognize when death is immanent and support both the dying person and his or her caregivers through the dying process.

Yet the duties of end-of-life care are also modest a great deal of the time. Caregivers make beds and wash hair and clip nails. They apply salve to dry skin and dress the myriad of sores and bruises frail people always seem to accumulate; they feed and attend to bathroom needs. They soothe by their company, their calming words, their gestures. They listen.

For those of us in some palliative disciplines little things are the sum total of our job description. I'm among that number, my modest goals consisting of relieving muscle tension to ease pain, to comfort, and to improve quality of life for the time remaining. Each massage is a one-time act whose significance lies within the moment rather than an effort to cure—a piece of fleeting performance art involving giver and receiver. That I attempt these things through a subdiscipline of complementary and alternative medicine (CAM) makes the efforts dubious in some people's minds. Although CAM has become more mainstream (and much more popular) in the past few decades it remains in the minds of many unproven, suspect, or outright quackery. Few insurance companies subsidize it; some hospitals resist offering CAM modalities, including massage, to their patients. Dismissals can be emphatic. Massage therapy has "no clear biological or medical effects," argues one critic. Though conceding that touch can offer benefits for anxiety and depression, he warns that the profession is "rife with pseudoscientific crank theories."[1]

Admittedly, if you watched me at work in the majority of hospice massage sessions you might think I'm not doing much. The sessions look nothing like what most people picture when they hear "massage," a word that conjures up a serene room where a sleeping, artfully draped and positioned person receives ministrations while lying on a comfortable and purpose-designed massage table. I work in the patient's space, not mine. Only rarely is a purpose-built portable massage table or chair involved. Few of the people with whom I work could get undressed and climb on and off a table in the half-hour allotted, and even if they could the process would be risky and painful. Where it's possible I do move patients to a side-lying position on a bed or have them sit in an open-backed chair, but most often I work with them where they are, sitting in a wheelchair or recliner, prone on a bed. Not infrequently the chair or bed is wedged against the wall or in a corner, flanked by cluttered side tables, so there's little room to maneuver. If a shirt can come off so much the better, but even that's not always possible and I work through clothes. Breathing apparatuses, IVs, and other essential appliances stay attached, and sometimes cords are everywhere. Facility staff, family members, or in the case of private home session curious toddlers or little dogs can appear at any time. Telephones ring. Intercoms page.

Such circumstances, as you might imagine, limit the work that can be done. If preliminary information or observation suggests a particular spot that needs easing and the patient is robust enough, I'll use gentler versions of conventional massage techniques, kneading and stretching. If the person is fragile or expresses discomfort at the above, I employ the softest of pressures, cradling a shoulder, cupping the back of a neck, stroking the fingers. With those for whom any contact is painful I don't touch at all, just hover my hands above the skin as I was taught to do when my husband was dying of cancer, breathing comfort, wordlessly and tenderly projecting *You're loved. It's going to be okay.*

If the person with whom I'm working is verbally uncommunicative I might add music, since to have a stranger putting her hands on you for thirty minutes in utter silence has always seemed to me a potentially awkward situation. This is live music, courtesy of my own vocal cords (long-ago trained in university voice lessons, though dormant in public performance for the decades between that time and this second-act career). Initially I brought along a little music player but soon discovered that sickrooms rarely offer open counterspace or an unused outlet. And anyway, a live human voice seems to offer a distinctively comforting effect.

I typically hum rather than singing. Experience has demonstrated that concentrating on lyrics and massaging at the same time can be one focus too many for me, and it would be inexcusable to mangle the words of somebody's favorite song. The standard repertoire consists of gentle folk songs, spirituals, and generic hymns—unless somebody requests another genre for herself or her loved one. Such custom concerts have featured Irish music, cowboy songs, classic Broadway hits, Barbara Streisand and Joni Mitchell and Bonnie Raitt tunes, once even The Grateful Dead (see chapter 9).

So there I am, humming away and caressing the shoulder of somebody who's sleeping, and I'm getting paid for this. What a racket, no?

If you believe that, I'll inform you that objective research has demonstrated that even gentle touch can inhibit the production of stress related fight-or-flight hormones and support the production of soothing hormones including oxytocin and beta-endorphins. Touch can lower blood pressure and boost the immune system.[2] I'll tell you about a 1998 Oregon study where family members caring for people dying of cancer were given massages. Eighty-five percent of those caregivers reported decreased emotional and physical stress; 77 percent reported less physical pain.[3] Even the efficacy of music has been established, thanks to the academic discipline of Music Therapy, a field complete with its own journals and advanced degrees. Research has demonstrated that music soothes anxiety and relaxes muscles (its rhythms and repetitions are held in particular to be very tonic). The way music is stored in the brain and linked to memory means that it can even stimulate cognition in people with brain impairment.[4]

What might be more immediately persuasive, though, would be to recount an experience with Ella, a sweet and silent ninety-five-year-old. One day last November I found Ella bent double in her recliner, her head on her knees with rigid hands protecting the crown, her only company a rowdy Hispanic pop music channel somebody had inexplicably chosen from the television's offerings. I turned off the noise, greeted her by name and reintroduced myself, and sat beside her on the little folding stool I carry with me. I began with Ella's upper back and shoulders, letting her feel the warmth and energy of my hands from a few inches away before settling them on her sweater. Since Ella had been a church lady and Thanksgiving was just a week away, seasonal hymns seemed appropriate for a soundtrack. I began with "We Gather Together," and "Come, Ye Thankful People, Come." The protective hands unclasped, and Ella turned her head to regard me with fuzzy attention. Ever-so-slowly she began to uncurl until she was sitting up normally, her back against the recliner, her head turned to the side where I was working, her expression a smile. As I moved to her now open left hand the right one reached to touch my working one, then stroked it in echo of the massage I was offering to her.

As the last song ended and I gradually lifted my hands, Ella spoke. "Thank you," she whispered. "That was really special. I've always loved Thanksgiving."

Fleeting, tiny in terms of the world's big picture, such moments are what we have as caregivers, and we must learn to let them be enough if we hope to persevere.

If discouragement and doubt come, it's helpful to remember that Jesus himself emphasized to his followers that they could best serve him by doing finite, small things. Three times Jesus repeats to Peter that the best way to demonstrate love for him is to "feed" or "tend" "my sheep" (John 21:15-17). He offers another version of the same message just before the Last Supper. The Son of Man, he tells the disciples, will separate the worthy from the unworthy (sheep from goats) at the Last Judgment on the basis of whether or not they fed the hungry, gave drink to the thirsty, welcomed the stranger, clothed the naked, cared for the ill, and visited the prisoner. "What you did not do for one of these least ones," Jesus councils, "you did not do for me" (Matt 25:31-46).

Thousands of saints, both the famous and the obscure, are distinguished by such ministry to God's poorest "sheep."

St. Peter Clavier bound up the wounds of slaves; St. John Bosco established schools for street boys. St. Vincent de Paul not only served with his own hands the poor, ill, and imprisoned but mobilized religious men and women and laity in this effort, becoming the patron of charitable societies; St. Damion devoted his life caring for lepers. Many saints better-known for other things—church administration, theological discourses, martyrdom, establishment of religious orders—were notable also for their outreach to the needy, including St. Basil the Great, a doctor of the church who also organized a soup kitchen and a hospice guesthouse furnished with doctors and nurses.

Today the saint probably most celebrated for service to the "least ones" is the twentieth-century Mother Teresa. Named at birth Agnes Gonxha Bojaxhiu, she rose from relatively humble origins in Macedonia to become an international symbol of extraordinary ministry to the poorest of the poor. Teresa established a religious order (the Missionaries of Charity) that began in India and had expanded by 1994 to encompass 4,000 religious and lay members and 600 foundations in 123 countries. She personally and courageously ministered to people suffering from some of the most contagious and terrifying diseases on the planet, including AIDS, tuberculosis, and leprosy. She visited the destitute in slums, washing their sores with her own hands, and traveled to help survivors of disasters including earthquakes and the Chernobyl radiation accident. In 1982 she brokered a temporary cease fire in the siege of Beirut and rescued thirty-seven children trapped in a front line hospital. The list of prizes she won is long, including the Nobel Peace Prize, the Albert Schweitzer International Prize, and the Presidential Medal of Honor. She was beatified in 2003, just six years after her death in 1997, and canonized in 2016.

Though this list of deeds and accomplishments makes Mother Teresa seem larger than life, in her philosophy and her faith she could not have been farther from a person who imagined herself a hero. No proponent of the grand gesture, Teresa insisted that the wellspring of her work was love, offered in God's name and for God's glory. She encouraged those who joined her to focus on practical acts of service offered with humility and reverence. "If you can't feed a hundred people, feed one," she advised. She championed simple presence, kindness, and attention. "The biggest disease today is not leprosy or t.b., but rather the feeling of being unwanted," she said, urging her followers to extend caring outreach to the lonely and the abandoned. "We shall never know all the good a single smile can do."[5]

How we perform services for the elderly and the dying may be as important as what we do, suggests a 2009 article in *The Journal of Gerontological Social Work* that is definitely in accord with Teresa's ethos.[6] The study's authors report that maintaining a spirit of respect while offering social and medical services is so crucial that it "becomes a significant psychosocial factor that affects the quality of . . . later life." Specifically, patients' self-esteem, reported satisfaction with their lives, and "sense of usefulness and involvement in community" improve when caregivers treat them positively and with behaviors that imply their dignity.

Demonstrating respect might seem like an abstract concept, but this report and others offer very concrete suggestions for how it might be accomplished. Some are obvious: dressing professionally, using proper manners, maintaining eye contact, not talking to others about the patient as if he or she were not there, etc. Other tips serve as good reminders of courtesies sometimes forgotten in practice, as with the simple matter of how we address our charges. As implied in the previous chapter, rather than assuming immediate familiarity by using a first name (or worse, a diminutive), best practice says to employ "Mr." or "Mrs." until invited otherwise. My experience suggests that titles, if relevant and known, are even better. How faces light up when a "Dr." or "Professor" affirms a cherished identity!

Studies also affirm the importance of acknowledging elderly people encountered in facilities even if they are not one's own patients. A smile and greeting offered to a stranger encountered by chance in the hallway of a nursing facility can improve mood, increase appetite, and decrease anxiety. I've been thanked, profusely, for the oh-so-basic civility of saying "Good morning, Sir!"

"Spatial respect" is also desirable: sitting on the same level vs. towering over patients when speaking to them, offering them a choice of seating if possible, providing services in a quiet, private setting (taking the extra few minutes at a session's beginning to wheel them back to their rooms, if necessary). As whatever treatment we offer is progressing, we ought to communicate with elderly people as we would with any other adult, asking questions that imply their continued agency ("Is there a spot you especially want me to work on today?"). We need to explain what we're doing, and to check in as treatment progresses. We ought also to avoid rhetorical questions if the interrogee in fact has no choice, for those simply reinforce lack of agency. "I'm going to turn you over now, okay?" I heard someone say to a patient last week even as she immediately got on with it, even though the recipient's look of panic made "not okay" obvious.

The list is long, but the guiding ethos is simple: do unto others as you would have them do unto you if you were elderly, confused, in pain, feeling invisible and powerless. It's so basic, really.

While working on this chapter I've been consciously employing these principles, and that attention has led to a number of wonderful moments. Working with a man reported to become easily anxious and hostile, I took the time to close a door and thus ensure privacy, and he proved friendly and cooperative. I asked polite drawing-out questions rather lapsing into "uh-hunh" mode as a woman described each of her numerous great-grandchildren during a massage, and her neck muscles relaxed more fully than I've ever before felt them do. Inspired by a conversation with Beatrice about fresh tomatoes ("That's what summer's all about," she reminisced. "I miss them so much! But here all we get are the hard tasteless ones."), I bought a few extra heirloom tomatoes at the farmer's market one Saturday and dropped them off in the kitchen of her nursing so that kitchen staff could serve her the fresh tomato sandwiches she loved. "Oh, honey," she said, her eyes filling, when I saw her next.

How many opportunities for other such big/little things, I wondered with regret at that moment, had I let slip through my fingers?

As I go about my rounds from facility to facility I often see a young man whose practice embodies the wisdom that great things are done not in the thunder and in the cloud, but in the whisper. Corey works as a CNA for the same hospice group that I do, supporting himself while going to college part-time as a nursing student. He's tall and lanky, soft-spoken and quick to smile, strong and patient. Though his behavior epitomizes hard work and dedication, the duties he performs would strike many as mundane, even disagreeable. He bathes people no longer able to manage their own personal hygiene (including people with paper-like skin and brittle bones, obese people, and paralyzed people); he changes dressings and cleans up messes; he clips nails and trims hair.

Such personal care ministrations can make recipients anxious, but Corey's patients adore him, just like he adores them. I was once lucky enough to watch him take his time finishing a bathing/grooming session with Frank, a large man with dementia. With great skill and respect Corey maneuvered Frank's polo shirt over the man's head and smoothed it across his broad chest, ensuring that it was not bunched or riding up. He combed Frank's sparse damp hair, gently joking with Frank about being "all spiffed up" for his massage. Frank beamed at him.

"What a wonderful nurse you are," I observed.

"Nope, I'm not a nurse, not yet," Corey countered, shrugging with cheerful self-deprecation. "I'm just a plain old care aide."

Frank's face clouded and he shook his head vigorously back and forth, not with the shakes of the condition from which he suffered but with deliberate intent. "NO!" he whispered loudly and with much effort, fixing his eyes on Corey's. "You ARE THE BEST!"

"Oh, buddy," the younger man replied, and bent to hug him.

"You know," Corey said to me as he turned to go and I turned to Frank, "Nursing is going to be good. But this is real good, too."

I smiled, thinking of the nineteenth-century French saint Therese of Lisieux, whom Teresa of Calcutta had taken as her patron. The former is admired as a proponent of the "little way." She assumed by choice the most humble house-keeping duties at her convent though she had been raised as a "little queen" by her family and her health was fragile, insisting that small practical services could be holy, too.

"I have never given the good God aught but love, and it is with love that He will repay," she wrote late in an account of her uneventful life of service.

To witness Frank's face was to see that promise confirmed—though in a modest modern key, brought down to a caregiver's earth.

CHAPTER 4

Reimagining Human Communication

Marion and I stroll around and around the corridor loop of the small assisted living facility where she resides, her arm around my waist like an elementary school girlfriend's, my arm reaching around her shoulders attempting to knead and stroke as we perambulate. On our third lap we draw curious looks from three women in wheelchairs in the central lounge. "Out for a constitutional?" one pipes up. "Why don't you sit and visit with us?" Marion shakes her head emphatically—NO.

As an off-and-on-again yoga student for many years I'm familiar with the concept of walking meditation, a technique that involves quieting the mind by focusing on the nuances of taking steps, breathing, moving slowly and deliberately.

While today's passage is certainly slow and deliberate, it's another sort of endeavor altogether, an expedient perhaps never before attempted: a walking massage.

Though some who suffer from dementia become more still, Marion is of the variety who want to move constantly, to pace and fidget as if the disease were generating energy that must be burned off or explode. I've hypothesized that this difference has to do with the innate energy level of a person's constitution, and Marion definitely supports that hypothesis. She was once a woman who "never sat still" in the words of her husband, Evan, a retired police chief who is resting in their suite down the hall. As the wife of a town official Marion effortlessly claimed the role of civic leader-qua society woman (if rural Idaho communities with populations of fewer than 3,000 can be said to have "society"). She organized the municipal Fourth of July parade, the Main Street Christmas decorations, the rodeo dinner, the Toys for Tots drive. She presided over ribbon cuttings for new businesses and gave speeches at high school graduations. She belonged to both of the community's women's clubs. In her spare time she raised four girls, golfed with enough skill that she won regional tournaments, rode horses, took a daily constitutional around the neighborhood, and maintained an enormous garden. Everybody craved invitations to her parties.

A decade ago, however, Marion's increasing forgetfulness was identified as the beachhead of Alzheimer's disease. Evan cared for her at home as long as he could, but eventually he and the daughters had to admit that she needed professional care.

We are having a conversation of sorts as we walk. Marion is mouthing incoherent words, leaning in confidentially (I think she just said something dismissive about those women). I try to read her expressions, the tiny variations in tone and body language, and to respond appropriately even as my extended hand attempts to relax her knotted trapezius. This reaching around is all I can do in the way of massage today. She refused to sit down for her session, gripping my arm and pulling me along with her. Nothing in my training ever suggested that one could do a massage standing and on the move; I'm making this up as I literally go along.

Nevertheless what I'm doing seems to be pleasing Marion. I lean toward her with what I hope is an expression of bemused agreement and she nods; that was indeed a complaint about something or someone untoward. She makes a sad little face back to match mine when I correctly read regret into a string of her garbled words.

Then I think I hear a wry, offhanded thing meant to be funny—though I cannot pick out a single word. In for a penny, in for a pound; I laugh out loud. "Oh Marion," I tell her, squeezing her shoulder companionably. "That's hysterical!"

She stops abruptly and pivots toward me, her face glowing.

Like any other person in her late sixties I've received my share of thanks over the years. Those related to teaching have come from graduate students completing dissertations under my direction, from teaching assistants I've bailed out of crises, from student writers triumphantly brandishing the magazines that hold their first publications. During this tenure as a massage therapist clients have responded with thanks as I've made the frozen necks to turn, the spasming piriformis muscles to ease.

But I've never, ever seen more gratitude than Marion's eyes hold.

Communicating with a person whose language and rational cognition is compromised, like Marion, is a new thing for me. Ten years ago I might have suggested that it couldn't be done, since for decades words were the medium in which I lived and moved and had my being. I insisted that my students use language precisely, that they pay attention not just to connotation and denotation but to rhythm and sound in their writing. As a writer I tried to follow the same standards. Truth to be told, back in the English professor days if you were a student who was inarticulate, grammatically challenged, cliché-loving, or tone-deaf to the power of words you wouldn't have received a very high grade in one of my classes. If you were an acquaintance and handled language carelessly, I'd have judged you (sad to say) and probably wouldn't have imagined you as a close friend.

Thus at the start of my massage career I found initial encounters with dementia not just professionally challenging but theoretically vexing. Could a person remotely hope to communicate with those whose ability to use words had disappeared, who appeared tragically incoherent? Was it even possible to be fully human without words?

Five years on into this practice I'm here to reassure you that the answers are decidedly, gloriously, yes and yes.

"The very word dementia inspires a degree of fear that 'heart attack,' 'stroke,' or even 'cancer' often do not," Mario D. Garrett writes in a 2013 piece about "dementiaphobia."[1] What Stephen G. Post has termed our culture's "hypercognitive bias"—our tendency to judge people on the basis of rational clarity of mind as expressed in language—enhances such a reaction.[2]

We are hardly the first to quake at the possibility of memory disorder, however: the "fear of losing one's mind" is among the classical great fears posited by Buddhist teaching.

And there's much to make a person anxious about memory disorders. Dementia (the word is a blanket term for a variety of conditions, including Alzheimer's disease) involves progressive destruction of brain cells, irreversible unless caused by a finite condition like a vitamin deficiency, a problem with medication, or a urinary tract infection. Correlations or causes are not always well understood; they include genetic predisposition, clumps and tangles of proteins in the brain, and vascular problems. Progressive dementia typically begins with mild cognitive impairment (memory loss, aphasia). Over time a person's language skills decline; eventually speech becomes incoherent or fails altogether. Sufferers might imagine they are in different times and places. They fail to recognize loved ones or imagine strangers to be intimates. They may experience hallucinations, especially with Parkinson's disease. Physical balance and coordination, reasoning and judgment decline. Those affected might suffer from depression, anxiety, trouble swallowing or eating or sleeping, restless wandering (like Marion), and dangerous or inappropriate impulsivity. Destruction of brain cells in the prefrontal cortex can weaken inhibitions. Previously decorous people may start using swear words or blurting out inappropriate remarks; they can act in aggressive, unorthodox or shocking ways. As physical wasting accelerates, immobility and unresponsiveness may occur. Death comes from medical complications including pneumonia, infections, dehydration and malnutrition, and thrombosis.[3]

Dementia also has social consequences since the prospect of interacting with someone suffering from a memory disorder can trigger fear and/or avoidance. Observers might engage in what's called "explanatory attribution" and blame the sufferer for his/her condition in an attempt to reassure themselves that this will not happen to them. As a result people in the early stages of dementia tell researchers that they feel devalued, dismissed, shamed. "I think that there is a perception that the disease is a personal shortcoming," one informant responded in a 2012 study on stigma and dementia. Many of its 2500 participants reported that friends had avoided them after they got sick or were uncomfortable with them, that strangers dismissed them as unintelligent or crazy, and that visitors including medical professionals treated them as "not people anymore," speaking not to them but to their caregivers.[4]

Even massage therapy students—some of the most idealistic, altruistic human beings on the planet—balk at the idea of interacting one-on-one with those in dementia's grip. Each year I give a guest lecture on hospice and dementia massage to students in the program from which I graduated, providing information and proselytizing shamelessly, but I've never had much luck in mustering new recruits. While the majority of these sweet kiddos are eager to imagine themselves doing disability massage, cancer massage, autism massage, post-surgery massage etc., they balk memory-disorder massage. "It sounds so amazing," one earnest young woman responded. "But I could never do it. It would be too hard to see people like that. It would break your heart to see somebody who is just a shell, with the person gone."

Thankfully for those suffering from dementia and those who love them, the proposition that "the person [is] gone" in dementia has come under convincing attack in recent years. Some of the arguments come from spiritual leaders and academics involved in the study of aging and spirituality. Rabbi Cary Kozberg, a chaplain associated with the Forum on Religion, Spirituality, and Aging, writes for example that dementia "cannot encroach upon the soul." "In my work,"

Kozberg says, "I see how alive and vibrant the soul can remain, even when a person's cognitive capacities are significantly damaged."[5] Buddhist teacher Thrangu Rinpoche similarly assured his students that although dementia damages senses and mental processes, sufferers retain their essential Buddha natures.[6] Pope John Paul II emphasized the God-given "wonder" of every individual, including those with dementia, and urged Christians to recognize "in the face of every person a call to encounter, dialogue, and solidarity."[7]

Research-based studies have afforded objective evidence that those with dementia retain distinctive emotional human needs, in particular the yearning for social connection. When given regular opportunities to interact with others, adults with dementia have been shown to stay physically healthier, to decline less quickly, to stay more alert, and to act out less. When offered the opportunity to take responsibility (as in interacting with children or caring for plants or animals), they become more calm, coherent, and outgoing. They remain responsive to nonverbal communication even in late-stage dementia, registering head nods, hand gestures, body postures and facial expressions, and responding appropriately.[8]

A particularly sweet example of how such a sense of continued participation in the human community can touch aging lives for the better exists at the Benedictine Monastery of St. Gertrude in northern Idaho. If a nun at this convent becomes ill enough with dementia that she cannot continue her assigned duties in one of the community's enterprises (retreat ministry, nursing, teaching, social service, etc.) she is listed on the community's website not as "retired" but dignified with the assignment "prayer ministry." In early-stage dementia these women can be seen in the chapel at all hours, praying devoutly for community members, their caregivers, and the intentions of friends of the monastery.

Even in advanced stages these prayer-ministry sisters are brought from the infirmary to join communal morning and evening prayers. They sit in the front row at noon Mass, smiling and peaceful—though a former music director does tend to burst out in spontaneous and joyful song when no one else is singing. They accept the Eucharist with reverence and listen to the readings devoutly. No longer able to join outwardly in community prayers, they seem to be joining within themselves. And even if they are not, the implication of their role as "prayer ministers" is a beautiful one: the very being of these aged holy women is a prayer.

My education in the craft of communicating with dementia sufferers has been best fostered by observing those skilled or unskilled in the practice. Affect is crucial, such examples have demonstrated. I've witnessed more than one person with a memory disorder become uneasy and resistant when caregivers were clearly nervous; I've also seen people melt from apparently inconsolable anxiety, panic, or rage to equanimity when someone who exuded quiet, confident concern smiled and took a hand or knelt and spoke gently.

These observational mentors have also demonstrated that if someone does become "behavioral" (a trade euphemism for agitated and/or difficult), caregivers would do well to attempt to identify and address an unmet need before assuming that the person's actions are irrational. Taking off clothes might mean that a room is too hot or that the person feels confined (open a curtain? unclutter a sick room? I've seen both of these things work). Spitting out food might mean that the person dislikes that particular dish. Rage and resistance can signal that a person feels invisible or abandoned and is attempting to claim attention.

Along this line I recently witnessed a psychiatric social worker quiet a terribly agitated woman simply by keeping her company. The patient was enraged because the facility where she lived would not allow her to leave to seek her daughter, whom she suddenly imagined was missing, and she became extremely disruptive, screaming and shoving. It wasn't hard to figure out why she was upset, the social worker explained later. "She's just terrified that she's going to be abandoned. Her daughter is the only family she has. Even though the daughter visits every couple days, Mary forgets. She just wants to know that somebody is concerned about her. So I sat with her for a while, and she calmed right down."

Empathy is everything, in other words, when you're dealing with another human being who happens to have dementia, just as it is when you're dealing with another human being who does not. Reading nonverbal cues, considering circumstances, and putting yourself in someone else's place can be every bit as effective a means of communication as words—sometimes even a better means.

Such basic sympathetic paying-attention facilitated my breakthrough with Marion. By the time that happy event occurred I'd nearly lost hope, for she'd seemed to want nothing to do with me. Whenever I entered the living room of the suite where she and Evan lived she'd retreat into a far corner, watching suspiciously as Evan enjoyed his massage, gesturing abruptly at the door, making anxious moans.

As sessions multiplied, though, Marion gradually crept closer. One banner day she allowed me briefly to massage her neck as she stood poised on one foot for flight. The following month she watched Evan's massage from her own chair rather than flitting nervously around the room.

Then, about six months into our acquaintance, I heard a tiny, tentative word as I lifted my hands from Evan's back. We swiveled toward her, incredulous, as it came again: "Me?"

Moving slowly, smiling determinedly, willing myself to exude serenity (*Of course you want a massage! I knew you would!*), I sat beside her on my stool, keeping my breathing slow and relaxed, touching first the neck she had previously allowed me to touch, then the shoulders, then the arms. All was accepted, and we both relaxed.

When I reached Marion's hand, however, it clenched into a tight fist. "She's just being ornery again," Evan remarked, but somehow the gesture struck me as more mournful than apprehensive.

"What's going on, Marion?" I asked. "I'll be gentle."

"You never know what she'll do." Evan continued. "Don't take it personally."

Nevertheless I reached to cradle the fist, turning it over oh-so-gently . . . and a fleeting glimpse of the little finger suggested the difficulty: Marion's nails were ragged and broken, the polish flaking away.

That day Marion was beautifully turned-out as always, dressed in a merino sweater twin-set and pleated plaid wool skirt that looked like something Audrey Hepburn might have worn. Her hair, though thinning, hung in a neat bob. Of course this elegant woman would be ashamed of unkempt hands.

"Oh, Marion, I get it. You need your nails done." She'd bowed her head, interposing a veil of hair between herself and me, but now she peeked out and nodded with a great air of tragedy.

"There's no rhyme or reason," Evan insisted.

"Men!" I leaned in, assuming a confidential girl-to-girl tone. "They just don't get it, do they?"

Abruptly Marion sat up straight, her mouth twisted in a wry smile. Then she rolled her eyes and cocked her head in Evan's direction.

"Hey Evan, when does your daughter come next?" I asked. The next day, it transpired. "Well, get on the phone right now and ask her to bring a nail file and some polish." "Nail polish?" He looked baffled. "Just do it, Evan," I ordered with a grin. "Now." As he picked up the phone I turned back to Marion. "In the meantime, let's see about relaxing those hands so they're ready for your manicure tomorrow." They uncurled and extended toward me.

And that was that—we were friends from that day on.

Trusting in continued consciousness is more challenging, of course, with people who do not respond or communicate at all, except perhaps for an occasional turning-toward, a subtle letting go of physical tension, a ghost of a smile on a sleeping face. To work with such a person—and continue doing so over weeks, months, years—is at once an ultimate test of hope and a supreme affirmation of faith in the endurance of the human spirit.

Agnes, to whom I offered massages in the first year of my hospice career, introduced me to that most reverent of practices. I cannot tell you how Agnes's voice sounded or what color her eyes were, since she remained always curled and silent in a fetal position. Massages consisted of delicate, static warming and cradling of shoulders, hands, feet, scalp. All the while Agnes radiated sweetness and gentleness, an impression seconded by the snow white stuffed lamb toy someone had provided to share her bed. Occasionally she would smile as I hummed an old-time hymn; once or twice she uncurled a little as I worked. Mostly, though, I kept her tactile company in the absence of any visible or auditory response, awed at the trust she was affording me, marveling at how intensely personal that wordless connection felt. I came away from those sessions certain that a sharing of pure sympathy, being to being, had passed between us. One afternoon alone in the room with Agnes not long before she died, I spontaneously made a little bow at the massage's end, pressing my palms together in front of my heart and inclining slightly forward as we do in yoga class. "Namaste" or "the divine in me greets the divine in you," the gesture is said to convey in Hindu custom, and that sentiment seemed absolutely apposite.

Agnes has been gone for three years, and since then I've ministered to more than a hundred others with dementia. I've worked with people in the early stages whose memories shifted back and forth from sharp to blurry; I've worked with people who were very verbal but completely confused and with those who were silent but seemed to understand exactly what I said. I've worked with people who were totally withdrawn. I've watched patients decline from the first of these stages through the last, to death.

And yes, I have to admit that my heart has often been broken.

But oh, what intimations of fellowship I've gained in return. We are all fundamentally connected in ineffable ways, this process has taught me, even though our physical bodies might decline, our rational facilities erode, our capacity for mere words fail.

Somebody's still in there, all right, and that being yearns for your acknowledgment.

CHAPTER 5

The Saving Grace of Humor

Though an individual who has never taken care of an elderly or dying person might consider humor an odd, even inappropriate topic in this context, I'm pretty sure that no veteran who has managed to maintain her sanity through the process does. Humor has long been established as one of the most powerful coping resources both for caregivers and for those they serve. Laughter stimulates the brain to release feel-good chemicals including dopamine and endorphins while reducing fight-or-flight neurotransmitters like cortisol that promote panic and stress. It improves the body's immune function, helps the heart function more effectively, and triggers anti-inflammatory mechanisms. It provides psychological comfort by distracting people from what is making them anxious. It helps them see their troubles in a new perspective.[1] Researchers have discovered that nurses and family caregivers who cultivate a sense of humor about their work are not only less likely to burn out but also to provide more effective, attentive care. Residents of nursing homes where funny movies and jolly activities are entertainment staples remain more alert, communicative, and even physically healthy.[2]

The kind of humor being considered in such studies, it should go without saying, does not involve making someone the butt of a joke—it's not mean, laughing-at style humor. Instead it disarms an unpleasant or frightening situation by bringing it out in the open and acknowledging its absurdity. It unites those who laugh together as they respond to something incongruous or ridiculous, sparking a moment of happy recognition—*we're in this together.*

Some resources for caregivers work on the assumption that benefitting from humor is as easy as summoning it on demand. When you realize that you haven't smiled or laughed in a while, one online newsletter advises, "take a deep breath and find some humor. Smile and inhale a dose of laughter because it is the best medicine." Joke books and stand-up comedy are advised as stimuli to "snap you out of being down," as are "silly movies." If those resources aren't to your liking, you're advised to try pretending that you're happy, either collectively (as in Laughing Yoga) or individually by "faking a smile till you make it."

If only the relief of laughter were that easy to summon. I like to think that I have a reasonably robust sense of humor (I'm that person who can relieve tense moments in meetings by making people grin), but a random silly movie or a forced smile has never been enough to turn an episode of misery into a laugh riot for me. When I'm feeling down, to try to force mirth from subjects unrelated to the day's context has always struck me as kind of pathetic.

What has worked to lighten my mood instead are serendipitous moments of laughter sparked by something that has happened in the course of real life. Such humor is always a surprise, always a gift, a wonderful jolt of sunshine and fresh air bursting into a day, speaking authentically of that day.

The incongruity (or script opposition) theory of humor explores the psychological processes that make spontaneous situation-related humor so tonic. Initially posed in the eighteenth century by philosophers including Immanuel Kant and Soren Kierkegaard and brought into a modern context in the 1980s by linguist and long-time humor researcher Victor Raskin, incongruity theory is based on the way that people mentally process the world around them. We habitually go about our daily business, it suggests, with a set of expectations about what things mean and what will happen ("scripts"). Incongruous events make us suddenly conscious of the predictive inadequacies of those scripts, challenging us to reframe and to distance ourselves from the original perspective. We laugh because our minds open to new possibilities of interpretation; we laugh at our previously flawed or limited understanding.[3]

How relevant this explanation is for caregivers! Those who tend people who are failing and/or suffering from dementia are primed by experience to construct scripts that anticipate only daily misery and fearful/pitiful encounters, to fall into a self-reinforcing cycle of hopelessness. When something amusing happens that disrupts such expectations, the person who laughs has been abruptly dislocated from captivity in her miserable script. She's been invited to see things differently, brought up against the reality that the world she inhabits still retains the possibility to surprise— and to inspire mirth instead of tears. She's reminded that she's a person with a richer repertoire of moods than her current days encourage, invited to inhabit, at least for a minute, a less fatalistic way of looking at things.

The circle I've joined at the coffee shop is laughing so loudly that other patrons are giving us dirty looks; one couple has already moved to a more distant table. These are middle-aged women I'm sitting with, not young people, but they're definitely getting rowdy, and I'm starting to fear that we might be asked to leave.

As my companions gasp for breath in the wake of one story, another anecdote begins. "And so the other night," the woman to my left says, "I'm in the bedroom and I've folded the quilt back and put the water glasses on the side tables, and Bob is still pacing. It's eleven o'clock, already, and I've had it. So I ask him, 'Why don't you come to bed with me?' And you know what he says?"

Anticipatory eyebrow raises and grins all around—*surprise us!*

"'I'd really enjoy that,' he says. 'But I'm a married man, and my wife would kill me!'"

Another roar.

The reality that a beloved spouse of four decades doesn't recognize you might seem too pathetic, even shameful, a revelation to share. Yet that very reality has just been brought out into the open at this table and there's no pity or shame in sight.

These women are members of a local caregivers' group organized casually by word of mouth through friend networks, random encounters in physicians' waiting rooms, notes on bulletin boards. They meet every two weeks in this coffee shop, lingering to consume an enormous quantity of caffeine and number of pastries (which may account for the establishment's tolerance). Sometimes a visitor with special expertise kicks off the session, as I did earlier in a presentation on comfort touch massage. The bulk of each session, though, is designated for sharing experiences. "Sometimes we do get serious," the organizer warned, "but don't worry—more often we talk about funny things that happened to us. It just feels good to laugh together."

You don't even have to be a member of an in-person support group to "laugh together." Whole websites and blogs and digests of blogs are devoted to caregiver humor. Niched sites focus on "dementia humor" or target people caring for their aged parents.

Only people like us would understand why this is funny, such telling implies it builds common ground, providing a forum where participants can confess and confront absurdities in safe company. One might even go so far as to suggest that such sharing of insider humor works somewhat like an alternative me-too movement. As someone puts a potentially disturbing thing into a humorous perspective and others laugh with her, the teller is psychologically and emotionally bolstered by realizing that she is not alone in the experience or aberrant in the response.

Professional caregivers have access to such communities through books of "nurse humor," websites, blogs, and, for the fortunate who work for employers up on the latest in best practice care of employees, regular in-person debriefing sessions where colleagues can open up and let their hair down with each other. In common with all occupational-group humor, the funny stories they tell in these contexts chronicle situations typical in the trade and depend on I've-been-there-too recognition and relief.

I was fortunate enough to be welcomed to the profession of end-of-life care with a delightful example of this genre, offered by hospice volunteer and Benedictine nun Elizabeth, my spiritual director. Elizabeth knows that I look up to her and am prone to perfectionism, so, like the thoughtful and merry woman she is, she told a story on herself in our initial meeting after I began my duties to encourage me to take the work and myself a little less seriously. Elizabeth described how she'd been meeting biweekly for several years with an

elderly woman who was falling ever deeper into dementia, checking on the latter's material well-being, giving her
communion, and praying with her. They got along well; the
woman seemed grateful for the continued connection to the
church and told Elizabeth that the visits were "very special
to me." Elizabeth was, in her own words, "feeling pretty
darned good about the whole thing."

During the span of that relationship the Catholic liturgical reform of 2013 took place, an initiative that revised
the Latin translation of some parts of the Mass, particularly the wording of the Nicene Creed ("one in being with
the Father" became "consubstantial with the Father," for
example). Since her patient was fragile and by that point
easily confused, Elizabeth decided to dispense with theological explanations and simply pray the texts in their new
versions. All went smoothly, though the woman did fall
silent during the Creed. At the time Elizabeth didn't give
that occurrence much thought, since her charge had been
growing increasingly withdrawn and easily tired over the
past months, dropping out of other recitations in which
she'd long participated.

On the next visit, however, Elizabeth found her patient
not withdrawn but alert and unusually enthusiastic in greeting her.

"Oh honey," the woman exclaimed. "I'm so glad to see
you! That girl who came the last time didn't know her
prayers!"

Humor, best-selling Jesuit writer James Martin insists,
should be seen as an essential component of spiritual life,
promoting holy and necessary humility (as the event just

recounted did for Elizabeth). "All of us can get puffed up," he affirms in *Between Heaven and Mirth*. When we tell jokes on ourselves, we deflate our egos, affirming that we are not inevitably in control. "Humor brings us back down to earth and reminds us of our place in God's universe," he counsels. Everybody needs to be reminded periodically that they are not perfect in spiritual practice or infallible in the performance of their secular occupation.[4]

Martin suggests that such gently corrective comeuppances come as divine gifts, wake-up calls that appear just when we need them for the care of our immortal souls, and what happened to me one afternoon in the spring of 2015 offers definite supporting evidence for that interpretation. By then half-a-year along in my new hospice massage career, I'd found my stride and was receiving rave reviews from patients, family members, and colleagues. I could always calm people down, even the most difficult ones, those who observed my massages marveled. I'd started to believe that I could work with any patient and in my incipient vainglory caught myself wondering why other health professionals struggled.

The day in question began (just like any narrative that will become a joke about ego deflation does) with direct and enthusiastic stoking of the script that needed to be qualified. "Could you possibly add one more massage to the day?" the hospice scheduler asked. The prospective subject had suffered a stroke a month earlier and had been growing progressively distraught, making outbursts, seeming angry. Her daughter was heartbroken at her mother's unease. "I suggested you, told her that you're wonderful with everybody, that all the patients love you," the scheduler urged.

Of course I fit her in, and was encouraged to see when I arrived a situation propitious for another star turn. The woman sat propped up on abundant pillows in bed in the sunny and neat living room, a loving daughter and daughter-in-law attending her, soft music already playing. "You're going to love this, Mom," the former said hopefully.

It immediately became apparent, however, that success was wishful thinking on all of our parts. Though the woman in the bed tolerated my touch, she fretted, grimaced, mumbled. Her muscles progressively tightened rather than relaxing; soon the discontented noises had become constant. "You're not liking this much, are you, Addie?" I asked matter-of-factly, softly. "That's okay. Not everybody does. I don't want to bother you, so I'll stop now."

"Just a little more," the daughter urged. "Please, Mom, just try to relax. She came all the way over here, and she's so nice."

Nothing changed. "Ok, Addie," I murmured after a few minutes. "I'm going to stop now." As I do with everyone to whom I minister, I thanked her for letting me work with her and told I'd enjoyed meeting her. "It's fine not to like massage," I reassured her. "But if you ever change your mind and want to try again, just let the nurses know and I'll come back."

The woman in the bed said something emphatic but incomprehensible to my ears. "Oh, Mom," the daughter half-sobbed, "No."

"What did she say?" The younger woman shook her head, turning away from me.

At the front door I tried to reassure her. "It's ok, really. I came to help her feel better, and if that doesn't happen, well, at least we gave it a go. Some people just don't like to be touched."

"But she was so rude!" she said, and this time the tears dripped to her cheeks. "I'm so sorry."

I couldn't resist. "Go ahead, I really want to know. I won't take it personally, I promise, but I'm so curious. What did she say?"

She took a deep breath, paused, then dished. "She said, 'DON'T COME BACK!' "

My laughter rang before I had an inkling that I was going to laugh. For an instant I worried that the woman beside me would be offended by the outburst, but abruptly she was laughing too, both of us shaking in glee at the chutzpah, the utter freedom of being so uninhibited. "Well," she said when she caught her breath, "Actually that's nothing new. She's always known her mind, that's for sure, though she used to be a lot more polite. She's still Mom, I guess, only less repressed."

We embraced and parted with smiles.

That was not the only time, I'm embarrassed to say, that the Mystery has seen fit to send me an ego-deflating moment. There was the morning when in the midst of a massage that I thought was going beautifully I finally caught on to the fact that the recipient was reaching not for her sippy cup or candy dish as I'd assumed at first, but for the panic button that would call aides to eject me. There was the day when I found a regular client with dementia who really did "always love" my massages in her room rather than in the nursing home lounge where the sessions usually took place. I bent for the usual kiss on the cheek she liked to offer in greeting, but instead she shrank back, piping in a tiny and pathetic voice "help!" a plaintive cry that continued for all five minutes of that day's session despite my best blandishment. There was the man's-man in the Veterans Home who sat silently through the comfort-touch treatment I'd been counseled would be appropriate for him, only to blurt at the conclusion, "You call that a massage??"

Such humor "blows the cobwebs out of our minds," James Martin remarks, as it tells a truth and reestablishes reality. Just like the emperor-has-no-clothes story, it makes us realize that we've been pretending, and we delight in the sudden shocking honesty, feeling a fresh start.[5]

If each member of a group of people has been telling little white lies because she feared offending the others, the relief of public unmasking can be exponential. That happened in a knitting group I occasionally attend, one of those where everybody is always so nice and supportive that even the most inept or outrageous creations are lauded as masterpieces. Such artificiality was blown to pieces one night, though, by an elderly member. Long one of the nicest of the nice, her inhibitions were thinning at age eighty-eight, and when someone took up a square in red and black she cocked an eyebrow. "What's that?" she asked. "It's awfully stark."

The piece was a baby blanket-in-progress, the knitter revealed. The parents who would receive it were very progressive young people, and they thought the color scheme would be good for either a boy or a girl.

"Red and black, for a baby?" the elderly woman shrieked. "Maybe for a BABY GIRL?" Then she began guffawing in big, out-of-control gasps, and suddenly everyone else joined in her mirth, including the knitter.

While such unbridled honesty has not come to rule the group's meetings, a new catch-phrase has entered its vocabulary. Nowadays if someone asks for input on a dubious color combination, yarn selection, or pattern, she's sure to hear from at least somebody, "Red and black, for a baby??"

In all the anecdotes recounted above, such pretense-puncturing outbursts involved a lack of impulse control, the result of physical aging and/or memory disorders. Such a set-up is typical in the great majority of caregiver humor stories I've heard. Occasionally, however, such reframing frankness is attributed to someone who is declining but retains full cognitive powers, and in that latter context it can represent a profound and deliberate offering to listeners.

"So we were playing cards that night, just like we did every Saturday," my friend began. She and her two sisters were taking turns caring for their mother, who was dying slowly and painfully from diabetes, and this had become their ritual, gathering all together on this one night of the week. "And as usual she was taking us to the cleaners, even at ten cents a point. We didn't let her, understand. She's just always been real good at cards."

"Oh, Mom," she reported that one of her sisters said when bed time arrived and the game ended. "You're bankrupting us!"

"Well," her mother said with a gentle "and kind of mischievous" smile, "maybe you'll feel better if you look at it this way: just think of this as a very short-term loan."

"We were stunned," my friend said. "It went completely quiet for a minute. Then Mom burst out laughing, and suddenly we all were laughing, and we were hugging her and each other, so relieved to be able to get this out into the open. We'd been trying so hard not to upset her by talking about death, but she let us know she'd made her peace with what was going on and wasn't afraid to talk about it. What a gift she gave us! What a relief! Our wonderful funny Mom was going into the hereafter just the way she'd lived—with a wonderful sense of humor and thinking about us instead of about herself."

Our capacity for humor is a gift from God, the writer/minister/comedienne Susan Sparks has said, a quality that mirrors the nature of a creator who delights in his work.[6]

What a sign of God's love it is that we have been thus endowed. Thanks to humor, even in the most difficult trials of our mortality we retain the ability mentally to put earthly difficulties into perspective. We benefit good naturedly from healthy unmaskings that call us to change our attitudes or our ways.

You can't be afraid and laugh at the same time, it's often been suggested. Or, as Martin Luther and St. Thomas More both affirmed, the best way to vanquish the devil is "to flout and jeer" at him.

Humor is not an odd or inappropriate reaction when life's end nears. It's an essential one.

CHAPTER 6

Earthen Vessels

If there's a universal refrain about the nature of end-of-life care, it is this: such work is extraordinarily taxing. It's apt to push a caregiver to the limits of her physical and emotional capacity; it's likely to challenge her presumptions about herself and force her to reconsider what she believes. No matter who you are, how much love for the patient you hold or how extensive your training, sooner or later you're going to doubt your own capacity.

Social science and healthcare researchers have worked to understand specific causes of burnout, documenting in both quantitative and qualitative studies that people struggle when they feel helpless and inept, when the workload is too great and the support inadequate, when regulations prove frustrating, and when coworkers clash with each other. Certain personality traits have been established as likely to hasten and intensify caregiver exhaustion, particularly perfectionism. Study after study has shown that if a person holds unattainably high expectations for herself as a caregiver she's doomed to fail, and she will turn the frustration toxically inward, blaming herself.[1]

Communication and education are the best preventative and corrective measures we can take, experts say. Healthcare agencies should hold regular debriefing sessions where employees can gather and share information, encouragement, and tips. Administrators should maintain an open-door policy and work to address employees' job frustrations as they arise. Family caregivers should be provided with detailed how-to information, given hands-on instruction, afforded 24-7 opportunities to have their questions answered, and offered friendly supportive brief check-in phone calls from hospice personnel. Everybody should have access to continuing education and to counseling, if necessary.[2]

Beyond such institutional support, both family and professional caregivers should engage in self-care. Time off (or respite time for family caregivers) is a necessity, say the advice manuals. So is "treating yourself." What might be meant by the latter is suggested by the brightly colored sheets I was given as a new widow in a grief group a decade and a half ago: "Surround yourself with pets, flowers, and love!" "Take long bubble baths and get a manicure—you're worth it!" "Get involved in a new hobby!" "Stay positive and cheerful!" "Be sure you eat healthy and exercise and get lots of sleep!"

Despite such analysis and coaching, the problem of caregiver burnout remains serious and perennial. Estimates of the prevalence of depression among family caregivers run from a conservative low of 20 percent (twice the occurrence in the general population) to as high as more than half.[3] Burnout is so common among end-of-life-care professionals that it might be termed a predictable occupational hazard, as carpal tunnel syndrome is for those who work forty hours a week on keyboards. A 2016 study of more than a thousand clinicians in palliative and hospice care found 62 percent reporting that *at that moment* they were suffering from emotional and physical exhaustion, apathy, depersonalization of patients, and feelings of inadequacy.[4] One informant in another qualitative study remarked of burnout, "It's like heart failure. It's chronic . . . and it will kill you."[5] We can even contribute to each other's anxiety across the divide of professional vs. "informal" caregivers. Canadian researchers discovered that nearly all of twenty-three professional/family caregiver pairs they tracked experienced miscommunication and resentment and thus were required in addition to their primary duties repeatedly to negotiate power differentials and appropriate roles in the interest of providing optimum care.[6]

The individual narratives behind these statistics can be heartbreaking. "I don't know myself anymore," lamented a healthcare worker interviewed for this book. "It's like I'm sleepwalking through my days. Every morning I tell myself 'You LOVE these people,' but that doesn't do much good. After so many years it's just getting to me, I guess—all that sickness and sadness and tragedy."

"You know what I said?" asked another, a woman who has won multiple awards for her work with the elderly. "What I said when somebody asked me what my next professional milestone would be? 'I'm going to be a kindergarten teacher,' I told her. It just popped out and sounds crazy, but I thought 'YES!' when I heard myself say it. Imagine for a minute—working with all those little energetic joyful people, people with their whole lives ahead of them, excited about everything. I can feel my whole body relax just thinking about it."

Even my friend Anna, a woman among the most selfless and loving human beings on the planet, eventually broke down although she did everything right. When her mother was no longer able to live independently, Anna had the basement of her own home remodeled into an apartment. After the older woman's cogency declined, Anna hired a top-notch companion to come in during the days while she and her husband were at work (she's among the 17 percent of Americans working full- or part-time while also acting as caregivers).[7] She was so patient and skilled in attending to her mother's activities of daily living, so idealistic that early on in the journey she described helping her mother shower as "a reverent, wonderful experience, caring for this body that gave birth to me." Gradually, though, the responsibility began to tell on her. "I feel like I'm losing my mind," she confessed when we met after work for a glass of wine together, these days a very rare occurrence. "It's always some big crisis night lately. I work so hard not to show Mom I'm upset, but I'm so tired and sometimes I get short with her. And when I look at her, how tiny and frail she is, how much pain she's in, how confused and agitated she is, I . . ." [tears] "well, it's horrible to say, but sometimes I think it would be a mercy if she died. I'm a terrible daughter!" she wailed, and would not be consoled.

I became one of those broken down family caregivers a decade and a half ago, primed for the slide by several of those classic risk factors. Since Ford and I did not draw on hospice services until the very end (we did not guess how rapidly the illness was progressing), I tended my husband without the support and the reality checks that those skilled in this craft could have provided. I knew nothing about the mechanics and theory of comforting someone with a terminal illness; I assumed the entire responsibility of caring for him, with no respites.

I'm also a stone perfectionist, the most reliable predictor of all. As suggested earlier in this book, I've always suffered from what pop-psych literature calls "control issues" (though I like my husband's phrase, "conductor's disease," better): the assumption that if something needed to happen it was up to me to ensure that it did. Thus when Ford's cancer was diagnosed I assumed in my own mind the responsibility of finding a cure, appointing myself as a sort of independent co-doctor and savior. In that pre-internet era and as an academic I turned to books, naturally (everything you would ever need to know could be found in a book if you searched skillfully and diligently enough, right? Including the magic bullet that would save someone dying of stage four prostate cancer?). In fierce full-mobilization mode I checked out every book in the public library that mentioned prostate cancer; I spent hours in the university library searching Medline. Before long I could have compiled a credible literature review.

But nothing worked, not the radiation, chemotherapy, brachytherapy, and clinical trials that the doctors provided, nor the qi gong, diet engineering, color breathing, visualization, love or prayer that I brought to the fight. After eighteen months my husband was released from attempts at cure and sent home to die.

I believed with all my heart that I'd missed some obvious thing I should have done or had failed to do, though that belief seems crazy in retrospect. During the last months of Ford's life such guilt was compounded by new unpleasantness between us, which I took to indicate criminal, unnatural failures of compassion on my part. Nobody had informed me that chemotherapy could change people's personalities, making them hyper-irritable and mean (you're welcome, if you're a family caregiver and nobody has told you that either). I was always either "hovering" too much or too inattentive, too hopeful or too pessimistic, too talky or too silent. *Anger releases the hormones that accelerate the growth of prostate cancer*, I remembered from some dubious book. *You're killing him.* At the nadir I imagined that I'd actually caused his cancer. Our meals had been too rich, our wine too abundant. I should have found a way to help him be less anxious about work. We shouldn't ever have quarreled. The epitome of that period's insanity was that I managed to discount the fact that both Ford's father and his grandfather had died of prostate cancer.

"Insanity" also seems an appropriate term for the ways I punished myself after his death through a series of accidents. Just one month into widowhood I closed the middle finger of my right hand in a car door, shattering its tip so conclusively that I might have lost the digit. Fortunately that catastrophe was averted by skilled plastic surgery and the insertion of a metal stabilizing pin that had me—appropriately enough—giving the world the bird all through the first bitter summer of my widowhood. At Christmas I slipped on the ice in my backyard and fell, bruising and fracturing ribs. I kept breaking household objects as if participating in an involuntary potlatch of earthly divesture—a favorite bowl shattered, a long-loved book soaked after being forgotten on the deck. I took up sleepwalking for the first and only time in my life, and during oblivious night wanderings I threw away the essential tools of everyday life. If in the morning I could not find the car keys, the little case holding my contact lenses in their hydrating fluid, a credit card, my favorite earrings, even once my grade book, the missing object would inevitably be in the trash can.

"Complicated grief," as psychological literature calls such a state of mind, is distinguished from garden-variety grief by its duration and by the seriousness of its attendant physical and mental health problems. Between 10 and 20 percent of bereaved people are said to suffer from this condition, which, according to a 2016 research study, is particularly prevalent among caregivers who experience "regret in relation to . . . decision-making responsibilities and outcomes" (aka, me). Complicated grief can morph into a debilitating, life-changing condition, leading to long-term clinical depression or other chronic mental illness, self-imposed isolation and deterioration of existing relationships, substance abuse, suicide, and/or yes, self-punishing "accidents" of the sort described above.[8]

Even if one's grief is "uncomplicated," the bottom line is that basically nobody passes completely unscathed through the process of providing informal end-of-life care. Common responses involve physical and mental exhaustion, sleep disorders, anger and loss of temper, difficulty concentrating, lack of energy, diminishment of interest in a job or avocation. The stress of caring for someone can lead to back pain and headache. The physical demands can cause injuries as a caregiver sacrifices her own body to the cause (as one of my studio massage clients experienced when she pulled the end of her right bicep off the bone trying to lift her husband just a week before he died). The longer the care continues, the more likely the caregiver is to succumb to "compassion fatigue," a state of apathy, helplessness and hopelessness, and perceived isolation.[9]

And those bubble baths and that healthy food and all that positive thinking, I'm here to tell you, didn't do all that much good at all, at least in my case.

So how does any caregiver, particularly one suffering from corrosive guilt, make it out alive? Since the initial stage of the self-healing process took a decade for me, I'm not the one to preach. Still, in the interest of perhaps helping someone else as stuck as I was, I'll tell you about the things that helped foster my evolution from self-hating new widow to reasonably well-adjusted survivor.

Just as conventional wisdom says, time was the most basic balm. After a while even the most determinedly scratched wounds tend to scab over, the rawest memories to blur, and that's a mercy.

Reading helped greatly, too (not surprisingly for this academic). I educated myself about complicated grief and cross-cultural perspectives on death and mourning; I read others' accounts of loss and recovery. What I found helped me put my experience into context and made me feel less aberrant.

I also undertook the sort of spiritual searching that is almost a cliché of bereavement. "Illness . . . changes the rules by which we were accustomed to perceiving the world, and to being perceived in turn," a manual for end-of-life caregivers advises. As a result of that discontinuity, the authors relate, we search for new perspectives that integrate what has happened to us and help our lives make the sense we need to continue to function.

That search in my case first involved realms I'd never previously explored. I studied Eastern religions and archetypes (the Hindu goddess Durga supplanted Hester Prynne as my soul sister). From there it was a short step to ashram visits, where I discovered kirtan, the tradition of sacred singing that repeats the names of God. That meditative chant soothed me and proved, by a process so circuitous that it seems like it must have been orchestrated by grace, to be the first step in drawing me to the more conventional sacred singing I do now as a cantor at Mass and with patients.

Though I found interest and comfort in such esoterica, it failed to provide enabling answers. Before long I turned again to the Christianity I'd long espoused. I read for the first time its classic writings and explored its saints' lives. I sought out living wise ones, too, going often for comfort and fellowship to the convent of Benedictine nuns mentioned elsewhere in this book, and to retreats and classes in other places where I learned about such things as contemplative prayer, Old Testament women, Catholic history.

In the end I came to understand that this Christianity that I'd so long assumed I understood was in fact exactly what I'd been searching for. At its heart, I finally recognized, Christianity is all about grace, precisely the reassurance we perfectionists, in particular, need to hear. Human nature, it holds, necessarily makes us imperfect, and inevitably we'll let ourselves, each other, and God down. Yet such failure need not be a cause of existential despair, since the divine power that shaped us is merciful. "Who is a God like you, who removes guilt / and pardons sin for the remnant of his inheritance . . . ?" asks the prophet Micah. This God, he proclaims, "does not persist in anger forever, / but instead delights in mercy, / And will again have compassion on us, / treading underfoot our iniquities" (Mic 7:18-19). The human need for grace and God's willingness to provide it dominates the message of Jesus (remember the Prodigal Son?). "If we say, 'We are without sin,' we deceive ourselves," Jesus is quoted as saying. "If we acknowledge our sins, [God] is faithful and just and will forgive our sins and cleanse us from every wrongdoing" (1 John 1:8-10). Stumbling, on other words, is not evidence of particular personal loathsomeness but something that human beings just do.

What is crucial is to admit our sins and throw ourselves on God's good graces (or "grace," speaking theologically instead of colloquially), trusting that he will forgive us.

Catholicism gives a particularly accessible form to that process in the sacrament of reconciliation (once called "confession"). This is a public sacrament, performed in the presence of a priest. During community penance services in the seasons of Advent or Lent you prepare for that rite in church surrounded by a whole bunch of other presumptive sinners. Once the sacrament has concluded you're told to "go in peace" and supposed to stop obsessing about what you confessed and accept that you're reconciled to God. Brought thus into the open, sin is in a sense de-pathologized.

I know there's a lot of talk about dour depressing "Catholic guilt," but I'll say this: I always leave confession with a sense not dissimilar (though of course infinitely more profound) to the one afforded by having my teeth cleaned—full of joyful relief and resolve to do better, feeling like I've just been done an immense favor, offered a fresh start.

Paul's metaphor puts the case succinctly: we are "earthen vessels," short-lived breakable imperfect containers for souls. It's crucial to remember that these souls exist and God's light shines in them even when we feel "afflicted in every way" and "perplexed." We should never allow ourselves to become "discouraged," or feel "constrained" or "abandoned" (2 Cor 4:7-11).

That message continues to cheer me now that I'm a professional caregiver. It's allowed me to let myself up after I failed to ease pain and anxiety, when practice became so automatic that I momentarily forget how much I "LOVE these people." It relieved me on the occasion when I allowed myself to become so rushed and harried that a family caregiver expressed concern about my health when she opened the door, asking "Why don't you sit down before you see mother? You look like you need a massage more than she does!" I've always thought that among the worst things a hospice worker could do was draw attention to her own troubles, so at that point I felt myself the lowest of the low. Thanks to the assurance of grace, however, I was able to offer that transgression to the Mystery and begin again with heartened resolution.

I believe that this "earthen vessels" perspective has made me a better caregiver—at least I hope so. What I know for sure is that it has made me a more thoughtful cantor at Ash Wednesday community penance services. The responsorial that day is always Psalm 51, the ultimate acknowledgment of imperfection and expression of yearning trust. I proclaim its solo verses from my heart: "For I acknowledge my offense, / and my sin is before me always"; "Thoroughly wash me from my guilt / and of my sin cleanse me." The congregation joins in refrain, all of us coming clean with each other, intoning "Be merciful, O Lord, for we have sinned."

As our voices rise together in beautiful minor key, I look out over those assembled and sometimes glimpse the face of someone I know to be a caregiver. And when I do, I hope that she in particular hears the promise in those words. I pray that she might find mercy, that she will know she deserves mercy, that such mercy might help her bear her cross more easily.

CHAPTER 7

Other People's Lives

"And just like that, there I was, calling the cops on Christmas Eve." Kim's voice holds both outrage and amusement in equal measures—*who could have imagined*?

"Unbelievable," I commiserate, and then we're laughing together because there's nothing else you can do when you encounter people who act so atrociously, so utterly immorally that they seem like another species.

Twenty years ago Kim was a member of my Girl Scout troop, a goofy and energetic little girl at once perennial clown and constant peacemaker. In elementary school she possessed a significant and good humored lack of coordination. I've often smiled at the memory of how she lay in the snow after a gentle tumble during the troop's first cross-country ski lesson, making a big deal of flailing around, pronouncing "I'm going to have to stay here FOREVER! Now I can't go to Disney on Ice on Saturday!" even as her hearty belly laugh rang, inspiring the other girls to take their own ineptitude more lightly.

Now in her thirties (how can that be?) Kim has turned into a very fine geriatric nurse, the sort mentioned in obituaries ("Special thanks to Kim of River-Sky Home Health and Hospice for treating Dad like her own father. We will always be grateful."). Though it felt a little odd initially to be contacting her as an expert informant, on this lunch date we've quickly, comfortably settled into a relaxed interview as old friends, equals.

We've come to the "challenges" part of the conversation, and true to form Kim has chosen to cast what might be an appalling, even frightening story in a funny light. This past winter, she reports, she was caring for a woman dying of lung cancer who stayed in her own home because she was "suspicious of nursing homes." "If it was me, I'd have been more suspicious of what was going on there," Kim says, describing a tumble-down place with peeling paint and cars up on blocks in the hard-packed dirt yard, cohabited by the woman's two adult sons and their girlfriends, couples who came and went at odd hours and sometimes disappeared for days. "But, whatever."

By December the patient was failing quickly and suffering a great deal of pain. Where many families accede to morphine drips only reluctantly (seeing this expedient as the beginning of the end, the diminishment of personality), this family appeared not only accepting but eager. "That should have tipped me off." Kim gives herself a little slap on the side of the head. "Nobody has ever acted like that before: 'bring it on!' "

Gauging an appropriate dose proved a problem. "She'd be good and comfortable, everything would be fine, then just a few days later it wouldn't be working as well. Then it would go back to okay. Before long we had to raise the baseline. We figured the pain was getting worse or her tolerance was increasing."

Before long even a strong admixture was inadequate. After a CNA providing personal care reported that the woman seemed in severe pain, Kim was called out on Christmas Eve. "So I thought that maybe something was wrong with the bag hooked up to the drip, and I went and got another bag from the closet. No difference. Then I tried another one. Same thing. Then the light dawned and I put a drop on my finger from each bag and tested them. Sure enough—the bags were filled with water. Those creeps had been siphoning off the morphine and either using it themselves or selling it, leaving their mother to suffer. And there I was, just like that, sitting in my car around the corner with the doors locked, calling the cops on Christmas Eve."

I shake my head, appalled but not quite surprised, for I've heard similar stories from others who visit patients' homes.

"The things you learn in this business," Kim spreads her arms wide in an exaggerated gesture of amazement, "about other people's lives!"

Professionals in end-of-life care are preponderantly law-abiding, nice people with solid middle-class values. They respect education and hard work and taking care of oneself; they try to live orderly, productive lives that contribute to the common good. They listen to worthy advice and take responsibility for their actions. They're responsible, decent people who generally enter their careers assuming that just about everyone shares something like that same worldview.

Working in public health, however, quickly disabuses one of *that* notion.

"I had no idea I lived in a cocoon all through childhood and college," a home-health occupational therapist among my acquaintance confessed. She'd just assumed others thought the way her family and friends and teachers did. "Sure," she admitted, "I saw a few people doing bad or weird things, but I thought they were a real minority. You work hard, right? You don't take advantage of people who are being nice to you?"

Such assumptions had evaporated during her first few months of practice. The occupational therapist was cussed at by the family members of one of her clients for being just a little, unavoidably, late; she was defied by a woman she was attempting to help ("I'm not doin' that, honey," the latter pronounced about an easy seated stretch that would have greatly eased her back pain. "I sworn off exercisin' a long time ago"). She caught patients who were on oxygen sneaking cigarettes. Her shoe was fouled by dog poop lurking under a sickbed. One of her patients' daughters manipulated her into going to the store to buy groceries with her own money "just to tide us over." "Don't ever do that again," her supervisor chided in no uncertain terms.

"I was mad," the therapist admitted. "I assumed they could smell the newness on me and were trying to take advantage. I was furious that they weren't listening to me." She shrugged. "But, of course, I know now that stuff like that happens all the time. You meet all kinds of people in this business."

You do, indeed, so if you're going to persist in home healthcare you soon accept that you need to get over minor affronts to personal dignity or taste. "Just let it roll off your back," one of my mentors advised when I complained about an incidental discourtesy. "Even Jesus walked away when he knew he couldn't change people. 'Just shake the dust off your feet and move on,' he said. For you, that means focusing on the person you've come to see, doing your best every time you go in there. As the counselors say, 'That's all you can control.'"

It's a different matter, of course, if you suspect that the situation is harmful enough to merit protective legal intervention, like the one Kim described. Or the one a social worker I know encountered. She was working with an elderly woman suffering from dementia who "was fine with me, a stranger, always calm and even smiling." When her daughter entered the room, however, the patient would tremble and wince. "I had my suspicions, but the daughter was always real nice to her mother when I was in the house. 'I don't know what's causing that,' she'd say. 'It must be the dementia—she must be really confused.' "

The social worker couldn't shake the sense that something was wrong, however, so one day she arrived early and approached the house quietly. What she heard through the walls confirmed her suspicions. The daughter was yelling, cursing, berating and shaming her mother; something crashed to the floor. When the door finally opened, the nurse found the daughter red-faced and panting, the patient cowering.

The daughter and the mother had never gotten along, siblings who lived at a distance reported reluctantly. They'd hoped for the best, but—.

A week later the mother was safely ensconced in a skilled nursing facility.

"I always try so hard not to judge family members," the social worker said. "I know it can be really, really hard to take care of somebody for a long time, how you're trapped. But that one was enough to ruin your faith in humanity, and it wasn't the only time."

How had she managed to carry on?

"That's simple," she replied in an echo of my mentor. "You always make the patient your main priority. Even if the family is difficult that sick person needs you, and your heart just opens to that responsibility. And the patient's heart opens, almost all the time."

She regarded me for a moment, thinking, then nodded. "But you already know that, right? You worked with Gil Duncan, didn't you?"

Though I came to healthcare believing that decades of teaching in an open-admissions public university had afforded contact with a representative cross section of the population—rural and urban, working class and middle class and well-heeled, members of many races and nationalities, first-generation college students looking for vocational training and those in love with the pure life of the mind, the hardworking and the lazy—the first five years of hospice massage have revealed that perception to be a cossetted absurdity.

I've been sent to streets and neighborhoods in my own town that I never knew existed, threadbare and sad places where poverty threatened to taint lives or already had. Notable among the latter was a filthy house where a diabetic slumped in dirty clothes, his recliner wedged into a cluttered corner, a Costco-sized jar of strawberry jam with a spoon in it at the ready on his side table. I worked with a man dying in a trailer house where the urine smell was so strong that until my senses mercifully deadened I feared I'd have to flee. I visited the Bedlam nightmare of a short-staffed "affordable" nursing home where people with dementia roamed the halls yelling, weeping, buttonholing each other and visitors with incoherent chatter, or lying dazed on the common room's sofas.

It was the Duncan home, however, that most disturbed me and continues to haunt my respectable middle-class soul. This was not a place of poverty in any material way; Gil Duncan's family lived in the most expensive subdivision in town, their house an enormous McMansion. It boasted a port-cochere looming over a three-story entryway at the head of a circular drive, multiple fireplaces, a spiral staircase, an enormous open kitchen, travertine and Italian tile, and decks that looked down over two acres of manicured lawns to a panorama of the city. Gil had his own "mother-in-law" quarters in an attached wing at the back of the house, complete with a large bedroom, a sitting room, a bathroom, and a patio that shared that view.

Yet the whole place seemed tainted by soul poverty. Whenever I showed up, at any time of any day, I found Gil's family—able-bodied adults all—lounging in their pajamas on the leather great-room couches, watching soap operas and game shows on a wall-filling television. Nobody ever seemed to work or to have any place to be. Ringing the doorbell roused only a shouted "Come IN!" necessitating the visitor to run a gauntlet of angry little dogs. The house held no visible books, no music, no evidence of particular interests, of volunteer pursuits, of making art or building things. Despite that magnificent kitchen there was no sign of cooking, either. When my visits happened to coincide with mealtimes the massage would be interrupted by one of Gil's children bearing a bag of fast food.

Gil's quarters did suggest that he had an interest, at least—in firearms. Trophies from shooting contests filled the fireplace mantle. A prominent photo on the wall showed the young Gil as a very tough guy, sweaty and gloating, dressed in camo and posed with an automatic weapon. His coffee cups and tee-shirts bore NRA logos; the bathroom door was adorned with a "This property protected by Smith and Wesson" bumper sticker. His personal enormous television set featured gun-centric shows, and I wondered what my massage school instructors, with their emphasis on maintaining a hushed and serene space, would say if they knew I was giving massages with "Future Weapons" and "Sons of Guns" as the client's background of choice. The room's pièce de la résistance gleamed in a fancy cabinet along the wall: a very long, very old-looking rifle. "That's shatterproof glass," Gil explained. "And it's alarmed. That's a real rare gun, a Winchester 1885 36-inch."

Despite his obsession with firepower, the Gil I knew was a consummately sweet man, polite and grateful, a man who remembered my name and greeted me warmly. "Thank you," he'd say, reaching to shake my hand after I'd spent thirty minutes working out the knots in his back. "You done real good, as always." Then, as I moved toward the suite door anticipating the pack of snarling mini-curs outside, came a parting formula as invariable and gracious as its content seemed unlikely: "Bless you!"

One afternoon nobody answered the front doorbell; Gil's children had actually gotten dressed and gone somewhere, forgetting or ignoring the appointment time. "I'll see him next month," I texted the schedule coordinator. Soon a reply pinged—could I possibly return later in the week? Gil had "chewed me up one side and down the other," his chagrinned daughter had reported. The only way to mollify him, he'd insisted, was to call and beg that I might try again.

"He's really fond of you," the coordinator remarked.

"And I of him," I said, marveling that this was the absolute truth. "Tell them I'll be there tomorrow."

During my short career as a home healthcare provider I've never been threatened or feared harm and I've never heard a substantiated story of anyone who was. All responsible home healthcare agencies try to prevent such things by carefully screening applicants and by training their workers in safety protocols. An informal internet canvas suggests that these are uniform across agencies: dress modestly and be prepared to move fast if you have to, keep your cell phone fully charged, let people know where you're going, park in well-lighted areas on the street rather than in a driveway, be sure that you have good directions and are at the right house, etc.[1]

Though a dedicated observer of these precautions I've been occasionally daunted by the prospect of entering a particular house. One afternoon last summer I drove three times by a peeling single-wide trailer in a marginal neighborhood. The residence was crooked on its foundation, its front-porch windows cracked and insulated with newspaper, the little metal front gate swing broken on its hinges and sporting a "Beware of Dog" notice adorned with a Rottweiler silhouette. *Please God, don't let that be the one.*

I checked and rechecked the address and the photo. This was indeed where a forty-three-year-old woman dying of brain cancer was waiting for my touch. Still, it took an interior pep talk to get me out of the car. *The nurses, social worker, aides come here all the time and they say the family is nice; nobody is going to murder or rob you.*

All apprehension evaporated once I got inside. The little living room was neat though sparsely furnished. Hand-crocheted afghans draped the threadbare couch and chairs; a life-sized statue of the Virgin Mary stood crowned with plastic flowers in the corner next to a tiny crystalline aquarium. This was a house of love, it quickly became clear, a place to which my patient had retreated after her boyfriend had beaten her, stolen from her, then finally abandoned her. "It ain't much, I know," her mother/caregiver admitted as she showed me out at the end of the massage. "But we keep each other good company. It's good to find each other again, even under the circumstances. Good to remember that we belong to each other."

And then there was Ed, who one winter afternoon provided a cautionary lesson I will never forget about making assumptions. "He's a character," the supervisor warned me when his name first appeared on my list. "His nurse will meet you at the door the first time and take you in to make sure he understands the ground rules."

The big old ranch house where Ed lived alone was cavelike, dark and smoky from years of cigarettes, bedecked with standard Western memorabilia—antlers, saddles, dying Indian carvings, blankets, rifles, old tin signs, rodeo posters and prize-winner's belt buckles. Less predictable—and hard to miss—were Western-themed soft-core girlie paintings. On the walls of Ed's bedroom bare-breasted Indian maidens offered smoky or perky jail-bait gazes, a trio of cowgirls in low-cut Western shirts and high-heeled boots leaned their thong-clad behinds over a split rail fence. A wiry grifter, truck driver, and bull rider who had once been a storied womanizer, Ed retained his appraising eye. "I can see you're a nice girl," he remarked. Then he added, as if he couldn't help himself, "and you're such a cute little thing!"

"Ed—" Nurse Lisa began.

"I'll be good, girl, just foolin' with you two. Don't worry about this old dog!"

"Yes, it's offensive, all right," Lisa admitted as we debriefed at our cars. "But he's dying, and we don't have a right to try to reform him now, so long as it stays at the pictures. You just have to establish the tone of your relationship."

I did, matching the friendly but no-nonsense approach I'd witnessed Lisa using, and things progressed innocently month after month. Massage did indeed help ease Ed's back spasms and forward-bent chest constriction; lymphatic work on his legs helped mitigate the edema caused by congestive heart failure. "You're the best doc I got!" he would say as I packed up at sessions' end, shaking my hand with a still-firm grip.

Then came the afternoon when I was running late, nerves exhausted by driving in an oncoming blizzard. Falling barometric pressure and dropping temperatures had compounded everybody's stiffness all day, inspiring grumpiness and anxiety. Ed's bedroom felt like a closed-in lair in dim light filtered through falling snow.

"You look real tired, girl," he greeted me. "Sit yourself down and let me get you a drink."

Oh, oh.

It's not hard to assume the role of schoolmarm when you were one for decades. I drew myself up and declined firmly, emphasizing that I was working and had more patients to see that afternoon. The roads were bad, I informed him, and I had to keep my wits about me. We eased then into the safe territory of discussing the storm and past blizzards. As I worked I remained on my guard, though, extra careful about positioning and reach.

When the allotted time had elapsed I helped Ed move back to the propped-up resting position he favored, then said my goodbyes a little more formally than usual.

"No, girl, I mean it," he insisted. "You need a drink if you're going to finish the day!" I tensed, but before I could issue another righteous demurral he reached into the bedside cabinet and pulled out . . .

A can of Ensure.

"Why then do you judge your brother? Or you, why do you look down on your brother? For we shall all stand before the judgment seat of God," says Paul in Romans (14:10), and that's a good reminder for us middle class would-be altruists.

Still, you undeniably do learn a lot about other people's lives by undertaking this work. And you can also learn a lot that you didn't expect about yourself. There's nothing like going into foreign parts to reveal that you're not quite as unprejudiced or as magnanimous as you thought, as resistant to reaching facile conclusions. Coming face-to-face with those who are strangers in fundamental matters of class or habit can humble you in a hurry as you realize just how rigid your assumptions are about how people should behave.

In time, as uncomfortable revelation follows uncomfortable revelation, you might even be moved to grant the truth that Mother Teresa voiced: "If you judge people, you have no time to love them."

Who me? I'll have an Ensure, with a big glass of charity on the side.

CHAPTER 8

Strangers as Friends

As a teacher I used to enjoy watching students make friends with one another, especially graduate students destined to be one another's boon companions in a small cohort for several years, to ground and support each other through a passage that proves so challenging for many. It was interesting to speculate on what drew people to each other, what recognition of shared disposition or taste, sense of humor or values, personality. Often the attraction seemed almost predestined, an experience of *I know you* that smacked more of recognition than of conscious choice. I made a friend like that myself on the first day of MA work at the University of Delaware, a woman who turned as I seated myself for teaching assistant orientation and smiled at me. *We're going to be really good friends*, I knew before we'd exchanged a word. We still are, more than forty years later.

It was nice to learn in massage school that I still possessed the capacity for sensing commonalities in strangers. This time I exchanged *I know you* glances with women decades younger than I, women young enough to be my granddaughters. Nevertheless they became my support and I theirs in the vicissitudes of schooling and they, too, remain friends after we've moved on to succeeding phases of our lives.

The instinctive friendships that have given me the most food for thought, however, are the ones formed in recent years with a handful of hospice patients. Naturally I'm friendly with all my patients, but I mean something more than "amicable and accepting" here. I'm speaking of the sort of connections where you understand each other so naturally, so absolutely that you seem members of the same tribe, the kind of friendship that promises decades of deepening connection . . . if the other person weren't about to die, that is.

From an objective point of view these friendships seem almost wasteful. To reach to another in incipient friendship involves risk; to cultivate a new friendship requires work. Hospice patients and hospice workers understand all too well that parting will lacerate their hearts before too long.

Yet those of us employed in end-of-life care cannot seem to help ourselves from making them, even when the difficulties are magnified by what might seem gulfs of apparent difference between us and the new friend. And that latter circumstance in particular has much to suggest about our essential nature.

Arguably the most improbable caregiver/patient friendship I've formed to date was with Crystal, a woman with whom I'd certainly never have crossed paths had I remained an English professor. Recovering methamphetamine addicts do not appear in advanced writing or literature classrooms; former motorcycle mamas are not known for their interest in abstract thought or their studiousness. A woman in her early fifties dying of pancreatic cancer would have no reason to enter the university in search of a new career.

Crystal had just come to town (and into her daughter's somewhat dubious care) on the day I first glimpsed her face behind a still-secured lock-chain. "Yeah?" she asked, then turned to the barking pit bull puppy behind her. "Can it, Harley!" Once she understood the nature of my errand, though, that door swung open wide. "A massage! That's awesome!"

Crystal sat in the portable massage chair I'd brought for that first appointment, her little granddaughter and grandson playing on the living room floor beside us, the puppy sprawled sleeping. "I like deep tissue," she insisted. "My back and my hip are killin' me." Her muscles responded well, and as I worked conversation began to flow. "You're a straight shooter," she told me. "I appreciate that."

"You're really funny and smart," I complimented her in return.

Over the next few months the talk became wide-ranging, companionable. We lamented the changes that aging women face (wasn't it kind of depressing, Crystal mused, when you realized it had been a long time since your last cat call?), and discrimination ("they took one look at our leathers and kicked us out of that movie, and we weren't even high"). We discussed current events ("they're all crooks"), and the writers she enjoyed, a roster that might have been used in the previous chapter as an example of the danger of snap judgments (Alice Walker, Sylvia Plath, Billy Collins, Charlotte Bronte). Most often we talked music, and I was glad that thanks to my husband's broad tastes I was familiar with the likes of Bob Seger, Bonnie Tyler, and Steve Earle.

"So, I hear you sing to people when they're so sick they can't talk," Crystal observed one afternoon. Nurse Lisa had clearly blabbed. Yes, I did, I admitted.

"They've been really nice about not telling me my time is coming fast," Crystal said. "But that's bs. I know. So, I want to ask while I can: will you do that for me when the clock is running out?"

It would have been a betrayal of our friendship to put on a mordant face or lie, knowing as I did how unwelcome efforts at consolation or gestures of pity were to Crystal.

"Sure," I drawled. "What kind of music would you like?"

"The Grateful Dead." She shook her head and raised her eyebrows. *Duh! Of course you could have guessed that.*

So it was that I revisited the stacks of CDs that Ford, long a fan of the Dead, had assembled, refreshing my memory. I practiced aloud as autumn made the evenings darker, my voice floating out the open living room windows into the down-canyon wind, remembering how doing this same thing, with these same songs, had seemed to bring Ford back into the room that first winter after his death. It still did.

Thus I was prepared when the time came nine months later to fulfill a promise whose odds would once have seemed astronomically unpropitious: offering a solo command performance of decidedly uncanonical deathbed music for a self proclaimed "rough chick who made a lot of bad choices," a "chick" who was also a dear friend.

Crystal had already been hooked up to morphine when I arrived for that last session; she lay quiet and motionless, her breathing slow. Trusting that she'd nevertheless hear, I settled myself onto a stool beside the bed, settled the quiet hands of reassuring presence on her shoulders, and began. I sang words instead of just humming that day, words about wind moving water, about song reaching to vanished consciousness, about leaving a rainy earth and not knowing what would come next, about a fervent wish for passage home, whatever that might entail.

I don't know how you feel about the Dead. A lot of my friends find them jejune, and thus I may just have betrayed myself in your judgment as philistine in musical taste. Nevertheless I will attest, absolutely and without embarrassment, that on that evening every one of those words seemed both profound and beautiful.

Compared to Crystal, Jocelyn might have seemed on the surface like a sister just waiting to be found. She and I shared wholesome backgrounds and the absence of a rap sheet, higher education, economic privilege, habits of regular exercise and healthy living, love of the arts, enjoyment of crafts, and support from cadres of loyal friends. In actuality, however, regionally gradated nuances of "we" might have kept us strangers, for Jocelyn was a Mormon and I am not.

Granted, today that's hardly an unbridgeable divide. Though in the nineteenth and early twentieth centuries suspicion, hostility, and occasional violence did mark Latter-day-Saint/"Gentile" interactions in the Intermountain West, now most of us treat each other with respect and happily consort with friends of the other persuasion. At the extremes of both sides and in some circumstances, however, some people do still keep to their own, and Jocelyn's situation promoted such cultural niching. A stay-at-home Latter-day-Saint mom who lived in a suburban neighborhood so predominately LDS that a Mormon temple will soon be constructed there, she had little occasion to interact in ways beyond the commercial and superficial with those outside her faith. Meetings and events at the church buildings just a block down the street dominated her social life; service to her church consumed what time her family of five children and a husband didn't. The family observed strict religion-specific protocols not always followed by the faithful of that creed today. They maintained very conservative standards of decency in the music, movies, and online content they consumed. They did not drink coffee or alcohol. They worshipped together as a family in their home, led by Jocelyn's husband. Though Jocelyn looked like any fashion-conscious, well-off, beautiful young woman in her late thirties, she wore "garments" (special underwear for married people) under her clothes, and if she appeared in a cute lace camisole meant to be seen, it was always placed modestly over a tee shirt.

When Jocelyn was diagnosed with metastatic ovarian cancer, though, the wider world—including me—came in.

"This is our dream house," she said as she led the way to the living room, smiling like a child who still couldn't believe she'd received such a gift. She turned, gesturing with contagious happiness at the pastel walls, the cathedral ceilings, the family photos with everybody dressed in the same color polo shirts, the sweeping view across the Snake River Plain to far mountain ranges, the "Believe in Miracles" plaques she'd decoupaged herself. A new dental practice for her husband, she explained, had brought them recently from Utah to that grand hilltop neighborhood, to that house so new that the fruit tree starts in the backyard are firmly staked against the March wind and the plantings that edged the manicured lawn had not filled in. "I have so many plans," she proclaimed. "I *will* beat this."

Despite such hopeful bravery Jocelyn appeared a very sick woman even at that initial massage appointment. Her skin was grey; athletic leanness had turned to gauntness. The ponytail did not disguise the thinning of her wavy long blonde hair. She winced as she climbed onto the portable table, and we had to do her massage side-lying because her stomach was so tender.

In this case as with Crystal, however, the talk came naturally. Jocelyn's "plans" included major gardening, and when she discovered that I'd avidly grown things in southern Idaho for decades she picked my brain about what tomato varieties would do well in those brand new raised beds during the impending summer, which perennials would flourish at 5,000 feet. Since the hospice supervisor had told her I'd been an English professor and was a writer, she enthused about the marvelous letters her oldest son was sending home from his church mission in Eastern Europe. He had real talent, she said, and she wanted to encourage that. Could he take creative writing courses while doing an engineering major at the university? Whom did I recommend for teachers? What kind of writing could he do in the meantime to push himself? And, please, could I bring one of the books I'd written next time? She was always looking for new things to read.

I asked about her daughter in high school, and we commiserated about how girls tend to drift away as teens. "But they come back," I assured her, citing the example of my oldest goddaughter, once a rebel and now a third-year medical student. "You just have to keep letting them know you love them and praising them for ways they're still being their own wonderful selves. You have to trust all the work you've put in and keep putting it in even when it seems thankless." *What nerve*, I chided myself. *You, who have never borne a child, giving this ubermother advice?* She listened thoughtfully nonetheless and said she'd needed to hear those words. What a morning she'd had before her daughter left for school! All that rebellion, all that acting out!

The next massage, Jocelyn insisted, should be in my studio. "I want the fancy lift table and the cushioned heating pad and the music and the flowers from now on, instead of you having to come all the way up here. It sounds so beautiful and peaceful."

A month of twice-weekly studio massages followed, and somewhere in there Jocelyn began calling me "girlfriend." Somewhere in there we also began sharing deeper confidences, and eventually Joselyn confessed how sick she felt. "It's getting so I'm not sure I'll make it anymore," she admitted. "But I'm not telling Jake or the kids. Just you, because I have to get it out to somebody. And we can still believe, right? I'm not giving up."

By early May this precious new friend had become markedly more frail. Neighbors drove her to appointments, and it was only in their skeptical looks that inquired *how do you know HER?* that made me remember we were on different sides of a local cultural divide. After the day Jocelyn was too sick to get out of someone's minivan, the sessions reverted to house calls.

One afternoon as the tiny backyard trees unfolded their first-ever buds I sat beside the hospital bed where Jocelyn now spent her days and sensed from her even more translucent skin, from the new pain that had spread to her side, and from her cloudy eyes that this might be our last meeting. Too lethargic for conversation, she slept. That day it was with particular reverence that I moved my fingertips in slow soft circular strokes down her neck, her shoulders, her arms, her hands, then back up again, finally cradling her head for a long time between my palms, breathing peace. "Love you, girlfriend," I whispered. "See you again after a while."

What inspires us to move toward each other? What sparks the instinctive *I know you!* that chooses this stranger rather than that one as a friend?

I cannot tell you that. What I can assure you thanks to hospice experience, though, is that the impulse to reach to others as friends seems to become stronger as time on earth shortens. More often than you might think, people who in their prime would have stayed aloof from each other thanks to habitual restraint or prejudice surrender to the longing for human connection, drawing together in the precious last span of months or days.

The example of one of my patients suggests that such bonding can be very strong indeed, especially if those becoming friends are mutually nearing death. The woman in question, ninety-five, came to our town as an utter stranger, moving from three hundred miles away to a facility near her daughter's home. She'd reportedly always been "reserved" and hard to please; as she aged she'd become increasingly wary of those she did not know.

Nevertheless, within a few months she made friends with two other women also residing at her nursing home, adding herself as a third to what had been a tight cohort of two. Since all these women were suffering from dementia and spoke infrequently, it's difficult to imagine how they initially communicated and connected with each other. Somehow, however, through some mysterious channel of understanding, they decided that they liked the cut of each other's jib and became inseparable. They knocked on each other's doors in the morning, strolled the halls holding hands, sat together at meals and activities; kissed each other good night. "The girls," staff affectionately called them.

One afternoon the facility held a routine fire drill, and residents of the daylight basement floor where all three had their rooms were assembled in wheelchairs in preparation for being taken out onto the patio. "Okay, Eleanor," a staff member said cheerily to my patient. "It's your turn."

Though typically compliant, Eleanor frowned, shook her head, and held up her hand in a stop sign. She sat up very straight, gathered her forces for a moment, then spoke.

"Oh no!" she announced, moving her hand to point at her most silent and fragile friend. "I'm not going anywhere till *she's* outside."

Stories like that are enough to restore a person's faith in human goodness, especially in these times of bitter division. They whisper that we may still, against the apparent odds suggested by contemporary politics, retain the capacity for remembering the essential similarities of shared mortality, the longing to understand and to be understood in community, and a common God-given nature.

The New Testament presents a beautiful narrative of realized human community in its depiction of Pentecost. Paul tells us that the event occurred in Jerusalem not long after Jesus was crucified, as apostles and "devout Jews from every nation under heaven" gathered. The Holy Spirit descended on them, working a dramatic miracle that fostered the development of the universal church:

> When the time for Pentecost was fulfilled, they were all in one place together. And suddenly there came from the sky a noise like a strong driving wind, and it filled the entire house . . . Then there appeared to them tongues of fire, which parted and came to rest on each one of them. And they were all filled with the holy Spirit and began to speak in different tongues, as the Spirit enabled them to proclaim (Acts 2:1-4).

Though those present spoke many languages, they were abruptly and miraculously able to understand the others, a fact that stunned them. When they asked what the phenomenon might mean, Peter evoked a prophesy: "'It will come to pass in the last days,' God says, / 'that I will pour out a portion of my spirit upon all flesh. . . . And I will work wonders in the heavens above, / and signs on the earth below"(Acts 2:17, 19). He preached the message of salvation through Christ, and three thousand people were baptized, people who entered into communal life, were taught by the apostles, and supplied the person-power necessary to spread the gospel.

St. Gregory of Nazianzus's "Oration on Pentecost" poses this scene as an antithesis to the Tower of Babel. In that earlier event, he suggests, language differences were imposed to forestall sinful collaboration. At Pentecost, in contrast, the Holy Spirit reunifies Christ's followers, "bring[ing] them again into harmony" so that they can spread his word.[1]

The wonderful litany of peoples presented in Acts underscores the scene's revolutionary nature in a political as well as in a theological sense. "We are Parthians, Medes, and Elamites, inhabitants of Mesopotamia, Judea and Cappadocia, Pontus and Asia. Phrygia and Pamphylia, Egypt and the districts of Libya near Cyrene, as well as travelers from Rome, both Jews and converts to Judaism, Cretans and Arabs" (Acts 2:9-11). Among these ethnic and national groups are those who were not merely strangers to each other (Cappadocia and Pontus were in Asia Minor, Egypt in Africa) but some whose ancient associations had been marked by suspicion or outright hostility, including Romans and Persian Parthians; Jews and Arabs.

It's probably futile to imagine that today in our tribal pride we might even want to speak the same language. Yet Christians pay tacit homage to that possibility every time they invoke the Holy Spirit, and Catholics affirm it in the Pentecost Sequence each year. The version my parish uses goes like this:

Come, O Holy Spirit, come!
And from your celestial home
Shed a ray of light divine!
Come, O Holy Spirit, come![2]

"Bend the stubborn heart and will," we sing; and "melt the frozen, warm the chill," words that apply not just to our relationship with God, but that are also relevant to our associations with each other—especially to fellowship beckoning as life's end nears.

If you're a person of faith, you might go so far as to imagine that our drawing together in such relationships— which any responsible cost-benefit analysis would suggest are folly—testifies that the Holy Spirit has never stopped reaching in, providing the spark to bring us into harmony.

You may even, if you find yourself folded into the precious warmth of such a friendship, dare to imagine that its joys ultimately might not be quite so fleeting, after all.

CHAPTER 9

Ordinary Wonders

From my earliest days of training in massage therapy I've enjoyed the mechanical rationality of therapeutic techniques. After decades of work in a field heavy on inference, theory, and nuance, it felt refreshing to be able to reach conclusions whose unilateral truth could be verified. If a massage therapist is conversant with kinesiology (the science of muscle movement) and thus knows where particular muscles are attached to bones, how they move the body, where they refer pain, and how they work in concert with other muscles (or in nasty cahoots when unhappy), she has a darned good chance of being able to understand why somebody is uncomfortable. Using appropriate techniques, she can address and more often than not mitigate the reported discomfort.

Such successes can occur with reasonably hale hospice patients as well as with able-bodied recipients of studio massages. Recently, for example, I relaxed the cramping side of an eighty-year-man who had gotten tangled in his oxygen-delivery system's cord while climbing a ladder to prune a tree in his backyard (don't ask). He'd stressed a deep muscle whose tightness was distorting his lower ribs, and after I'd worked the area his pain disappeared. The only downside is that he's probably already back out in that yard, emphysema, oxygen, and all, bent on accomplishing the fall clean-up he's always done all by himself.

More often in end-of-life massage, however, the breakthrough moments in my practice are inspired not from muscle manipulations guided by rational deduction but from what feels like uncanny intuition.

I've waited until now to talk about those latter occasions because describing them in company sometimes elicits raised eyebrows, attempts at quick too-easy explanation, or expressions that I understand to say something like *Poor Susan. She used to be a critical thinker; now she's bought into that new-age quackery.* But since you've read this far, I'm assuming with fingers crossed that you're willing to at least entertain the narratives of such events.

And to exclude them in this book in all their uncanny glory, it seems to me, would be to suppress one of the most evocative aspects of end-of-life care

Nellie was thrashing and moaning, exclaiming about a house fire, children, *lost*. Although neither her case file nor an emergency phone call to her daughter indicated such an incident in her history ("maybe she saw something on television, or read it in a magazine, or heard about it from somebody" an employee at the nursing home offered) the terror was physiologically real. Nellie's heart rate soared; her breathing gasped; her color was terrible.

"Hi, my friend," I said softly, smiling into those wild eyes, willing a barrier between my own heart and whatever contagious archetypal fears tonight possessed this long-time patient of mine, usually so serene and friendly. Her hand flinched and attempted to clench shut as I cradled it in mine, but as my thumb caressed the palm it blossomed softly open. I cupped and stroked her fingers as a group then individually, warming them. I worked up her arms and shoulders, humming the hymns beloved of the generation of Catholics to which I knew she belonged: "Be Still My Soul," "O Sanctissima," "Be Thou My Vision," "Hail Holy Queen." So calm did she become that I dared to hover my palms in the vulnerable zone behind her neck at the base of her skull, breathing coolness.

As I did, an old-time hymn from my Presbyterian youth flooded into my mind, "In the Garden," one that features scooping sentimental cadences and in my uncharitable judgment tent-revival-tinged lyrics. I'd never considered humming it to a hospice patient; it's not in any Catholic hymnal I've ever seen. The words sounded so insistently in my head, however, that I suspended my "no songs I dislike" rule and began to hum the melody that accompanied them:

> I come to the garden alone
> While the dew is still on the roses
> And the voice I hear, falling on my ear
> The Son of God discloses.
> And He walks with me, and He talks with me,
> And He tells me I am His own.
> And the joy we share as we tarry there,
> None other has ever known.[1]

I half imagined, at first, that I was simply hearing the echo of my own voice, but as the melody stabilized and matched mine, I recognized its source. Nellie was singing along with me, her eyes closed, her body gently swaying in time—singing *the text* of that hymn though I was not.

"Oh, my goodness, thank you." As the last verse ended I turned to a woman behind me having an obviously emotional moment. She was Nellie's daughter, just arrived from a town twenty miles away. "Thank you," she repeated. Then, "How did you know? That's always been her favorite hymn."

When touch and presence are able to achieve such relief I always remember the first time such a thing happened, that aforementioned afternoon in the spring of 2002 when these same hands went instinctively to the epicenter of my husband's pain and helped to calm it, though I was then a woman who believed that she possessed worse than no skills at all as a caregiver and knew absolutely nothing about anatomy, physiology, kinesiology.

As somebody who now lays hands on people for a living, I'm happy to say that formal training has not interfered with that more spontaneous capacity for knowing where and how to comfort, nor has it diminished the sense of awe it inspires. My hands continue to find areas of pain or tension of which nurses are unaware and that confused or uncommunicative patients can't clearly report—a pulsating core of a headache, a point on the outside of a leg that was causing a foot cramp. Such ministrations regularly inspire the easing of muscles, the relaxing of a brow, the opening of eyes in a smile.

I want to be clear: I'm not claiming shamanic efficacy. I don't believe that I possess a magical power and that I can summon this healing on demand. On certain days the intuitive knowing simply appears as a sense of a pulsing persistent flow, rippling in through the top of my head and flowing down and out through my palms and fingers, a tonic force. "Your hands are so warm!" those with whom I work comment on those days. I never get tired when that feeling is running through me, never lose attention no matter how busy the schedule. Indeed, some residual effect seems to linger in my own cells and psyche, calming me as the hours pass, filling me with contentment. Although I have trouble sleeping on other nights, the most peaceful and sustained slumber imaginable closes the days in question.

If this practice were described to someone familiar with holistic medicine, she'd call it "energy work." A major health trend, energy work is a category of treatment modalities based on the premise that the human body contains a field of force. Illness and emotional/psychological problems come when that field is disrupted, it is said; practitioners seek to unblock and/or rebalance its flow.[2]

Though the concept might seem fluffy and faddish, health-care modalities that purport to employ energy have been respected for centuries in other cultures, including Traditional Chinese medicine, with its disciplines of acupressure and acupuncture, and Indian Ayurvedic medicine. In contemporary America some forms of energy medicine are used in hospitals and taught in nursing schools.[3] Variations on the theme employed by massage therapists include Therapeutic Touch, Healing Touch, Comfort Touch, and Polarity. Reiki, a Japanese technique that draws on energy, is the most elaborate in its formal scaffolding. Practitioners are required to be initiated (or "attuned" in the discipline's lingo) by a mentor, then initiates are taught to summon Reiki Guides, "enlightened spiritual beings" to help them in their practice. As training progresses sacred symbols are revealed by the teacher, said to automatically connect the practitioner to higher consciousness when drawn, visualized, or pronounced aloud.

Not surprisingly given this cabalistic apparatus, Reiki has come under fire as a pagan practice. "BE CAREFUL of that stuff," a conservative member of my parish counseled me when she learned I was going to attend a class. "No matter what they tell you, only pronounce the name of the Holy Spirit. You can't trust that the ones they're calling aren't malevolent spirits in disguise." Though the latter parts of that caution seemed like something out of the Middle Ages, I discovered that she was actually referencing a 2009 document by the US Conference of Catholic Bishops that branded Reiki as contrary to church teaching. Besides the potentially dubious nature of those spirit guides, the core sticking point in the bishops' mind was all that talk about "automatic" connection with higher powers and guaranteed healing. "For the Reiki practitioner, the healing power is at human disposal," the bishops write; thus God's authority has been usurped.[4]

Neither the woman who warned me nor the bishops had any cause to worry about me, it turns out. Though I completed that class I've never practiced formal Reiki. All that talk about spirit guides and secret symbols just seemed silly to me—and unnecessary. I'd learned by then that I didn't need an esoteric connection to a source of healing with an ancient sounding name (or an even more skepticism-inducing everyday American nickname—I once met a woman practicing Reiki who credited "Barb" and "Toni" with helping her work miracles). I wasn't interested in magic words.

After all, I'd already reaffirmed trust in the ubersource of comfort and healing through the process of making peace again after Ford's death, and through the evolution of calling to new vocation. "I will restore your health; / I will heal your injuries . . . says the LORD," Jeremiah comforts his listeners (30:17). Such words encompass physical as well as spiritual healing. God can bind up wounds (Ps 147:3), the Bible affirms, calm trembling bones (Ps 7:3), and address depression and mental illness by healing broken hearts (Ps 147:3). Jesus cures literal blindness, leprosy, and mental illness in the name of the divine, and witnesses recognize God's power as the source of the healing. After the cure of the crippled man, Matthew tells us, the crowds "were struck with awe and glorified God who had given such authority to human beings" (9:8).

Those of us who find ourselves able to soothe others' anxiety and pain—whether through sympathetic touch or by more conventional medical procedures—would do well to consider that we, too, might be drawing on "authority" not of our own making. Paul implicitly encourages such a perspective when speaking of God as the source of all human talents. We must bear in mind that we are mere branches on the tree; it is "the root that sustains us." "So do not become haughty, but stand in awe," he cautions. "I do not want you to be unaware of this mystery . . . so that you will not become wise [in] your own estimation" (Rom 11:17-25).

I work hard to keep these humbling words in mind as I quietly go about my practice, delighting in the holy and breathtaking not-me force when it appears, trusting in Paul's "by their fruits you shall know them" principle when my hands afford healing that surprises me rather than worrying about malevolent spirits in disguise.[5] I always give thanks. If the Mystery chooses to be somewhere else on a particular day and I'm left to my own devices, I rely instead on analysis, training, and conscious sympathies, and they usually work well enough.

And that, I've discovered, isn't a bad formula for how to live one's life in general.

Many others in this business of end-of-life care report that they, too, have felt what seemed to be the touch of holy guidance. It doesn't seem to matter what particular creed one espouses. I've heard stories of mysterious intuition from Christians of all stripes and from those who profess other spiritual traditions, including a good and ethical woman who self-identifies as a Wiccan.

Some of these accounts involve practitioners knowing things that they could not have known, as with my own experience with Nellie. One of the most striking among them is the story told by a hospice volunteer about a day of ministry that began with gathering flowers from her garden to distribute on her rounds. Usually this woman culled sturdy blooms that would last a week, at least, after cutting—daisies and marigolds and zinnias, bachelors' buttons, and sunflowers. On that morning, though, she could not resist the urge to go to her tea rose patch. "It sounds really woo-woo, but the white roses seemed to be saying, 'Cut me!' even though they're the most fragile ones." The vase with those particular flowers ended up in the room of a first-time patient, a woman sleeping soundly when she arrived. "They told me she'd had a bad night," the volunteer said. "And those roses seemed to belong there, for some reason. So I just put them down on the bedside table and tiptoed out, thinking I'd come back later in the week."

"It was you, wasn't it?" The email from the woman's son landed in her in-box a few hours later. "The staff said you always bring flowers, and I wanted to tell you how grateful we are. Mom has always grown white roses and was so sad to leave her garden. She was so happy when she woke up and saw them—happier than I've heard her for ages. 'It was like the angels stopped by,' she said. 'And knew just what I needed.' "

Other healthcare professionals recount flashes of intuitive wisdom that contradicted apparent facts. A high-school-aged nursing home aide very new to the job told with amazement of how she "just knew" a man with dementia needed water. Charts showed that the patient had received the recommended amount that day; the aide had been warned about giving extra water at night because of "bathroom issues." But when the girl saw the patient tossing and turning in discomfort she heeded her intuition. She offered a straw, and the man grabbed it and sucked voraciously, emptying the cup then emptying another. He'd been severely dehydrated as a rare side effect of a new medication, it was determined when the hospice nurse came after the aide's responsible check-in call. If not given water, he might have suffered a seizure. "How did I know to do that," the aide mused to me, shrugging her shoulders. "Well, really, I didn't know, not like assessing or anything. I'd only been in the beginning pre-nursing classes for two weeks."

She paused, grinning. "Actually, this is going to sound nuts, but all I can say is it felt like when a computer guy is doing remote repair and he takes over your mouse and you sit there and watch the screen move around all by itself. That's what it felt like when I held the cup up to his mouth."

Among the most moving of these intuition stories are those from end-of-life professionals who report that they have felt a sixth sense about when "somebody is getting ready to go." One such reported experiencing a strong pull to visit a patient on a Sunday evening. He'd seemed just fine on Friday and the nurse was due to see him in the morning, but she went anyway. On that short-staffed weekend night she found him unattended in his room, gasping for breath, moving toward death. She made him comfortable, called the hospice group for support, and summoned his family. Thus he made the passage in the company of those he loved.

The events described in this chapter are not miracles in the canonical sense, of course. They do not violate or transcend the effects of nature. Nor do they necessarily indicate some sort of mysterious psychic power. It's a fact well-established in psychological research that professionals can read expressions and subtle physical signs without being consciously aware of what they're doing.

Yet I believe you'll have to agree that, at the very least, they offer substantial evidence that we have been "wonderfully made," as the psalmist says (139:14).

One of the most marked transformations that end-of-life practice has wrought on me is the willingness to acknowledge openly that I've felt the operations of what I believe to be the Mystery's guidance. Twenty years ago I might have written an essay like this (for I've long imagined that I sensed the Mystery's touch), but it would have been full of apologetics regarding uncanny events. Given the experiences and intimations of the past half-decade, however, I'm content to stand now acknowledging that, as the poet Alfred, Lord Tennyson puts it, I "believ[e] where [I] cannot prove."[6]

That willingness to grant the touch of wonder in my hospice practice has had the broader effect of clearing the scales from my eyes in other parts of life. These days even the most ordinary of things can appear as crackling with grace, as wonders in their own right.

Such was the case with this year's annual June birthday hike, a workout that morphed into a celebration of much more than just turning sixty-eight. I set off for a solo exploration that morning (work demands were making me feel "peopled out," in Ford's phrase, though dinner with friends awaited), eager to explore the upper reaches of a mountain path I'd started up with others. What I discovered once I'd passed the previous high point was lovely indeed. The trail first entered a beautiful aspen grove, its sheltered north-facing aspect offering a tiny and distinctive ecosystem after the bare sagebrush mountainsides I'd been traversing. I paused for a drink of cool water, enjoying the shade, the soft grass underfoot, the wrens and finches flitting in dappled sunlight. Back out in the open the path grew steeper and more challenging, crossing rockfalls. Bright native sunflowers (artemisia, or "mule's ears") carpeted the canyon sides with gold punctuated by the blue of larkspur and lupine, the red of Indian Paintbrush, the delicate pink of wild roses. The trail's last half-mile before topping out at a high ridge ran sheltered inside a narrowing canyon, dark and silent in the shade of towering pines.

I stopped on that ridge, in a saddle between two tall peaks, and plopped down to take in the view of the little city that has been my home for so long. The appreciation of being able to reach such a place on a "senior" birthday struck me, and the realization of how unlikely it would have seemed when I was a timid girl growing up in suburban Philadelphia that I'd ever at any age possess the easy confidence to hike four miles and 1500 feet uphill on a new-to-me mountain trail.

So precious to be able to do this. What a glorious life I've had. I have.

In the sprawl dozing below in the midday sun I identified places where I'd offered solace to people nearing the ends of their lives—and would again offer the very next day.

I sent love to particular faces I knew to be behind those distant windows as I had to the college students on the breakthrough night in student clinic. I tried fancifully to channel to them the clean fresh air, the warm sun, the sense of spaciousness of this perch. I prayed for those no longer below, and for those whom I hadn't yet met but would be blessing next year on this day, God willing, from some spot of lofty mountain grandeur.

I thought, too, of the complicated chain of circumstances that had brought me to that place in both a literal geographic sense and more abstract vocational one. All alone with the ravens and the swallows that rode the ridge's thermals I laughed aloud, thinking *what were the chances?* but believing in my heart that they had not been chances at all.

CHAPTER 10

Mortality, Every Morning

It must be so hard to work with people who are going to die," my neighbor says when we run into each other at the grocery store.

This is hardly the first time I've heard this sentiment, and as usual I resist the temptation to point out that everybody whose occupation involves dealing with human beings does exactly that all the time.

Yes, sometimes it can be hard, I concede. But end-of-life care is nevertheless one of the most inspirational, uplifting things I've ever done.

She looks at me with incredulity. "I really admire you," she says. "And I know somebody has to do it. But not me. Thinking about death is the last thing I want to do. Especially since I'm getting up there myself."

"Thinking about death is the last thing" many people want to do in the twenty-first century, it seems. Not only are we in denial about aging; we're even more anxious about acknowledging aging's inevitable end, so anxious that our culture has been termed "death-avoidant" and "death-phobic."[1] Advances in medical science tempt us, as Atul Gawande and many others have suggested, to believe that death can be not just long-delayed, but perhaps even overcome someday. Doctors are trained to approach diseases as challenges to be conquered; if one treatment fails, another, more extreme strategy is always available to be tried. In such a mindset death is framed a failure on the part of the physician and/or the patient.[2] We use military metaphors: we "battle" with cancer and undertake "campaigns" in research laboratories to find a cure for dementia. Those who find remission are "survivors" and those who "lose their battle" are by implication people who haven't tried hard enough—a pernicious judgment.

As a consequence of such attitudes we "back into the future," in the words of Rabbi Zalman Schachter-Shalomi, "locked in a small box, resisting the flow of time." This denial can have dire psychological and spiritual consequences, Schachter-Shalomi warns, trapping us in "a shriveled-up present, bereft of past and future in a psychic field that mimics Alzheimer's disease." At worst we die unprepared, our energy consumed in fighting to the end. If we finally must concede that death is near, we risk ending our days with a sense of betrayal, an anger that gets in the way of making peace with this universal human transition.[3]

One of the saddest examples of this phenomenon I've seen in my practice was a woman who wasn't even approaching death at the time—she was simply paralyzed by having been forced to acknowledge its possibility.

"At first she was so happy." Marjorie said, referencing her seventy-two year old mother. "When they told her that the chemo had worked and she was cancer-free, she got so interested in life again, almost like her old self." As time passed, however, Marjorie's mother became more and more anxious. "She's nervous about every test," Marjorie said. "When the last one had a little possible red flag, even though that got dismissed as nothing to worry about she got so agitated. Now she's so depressed. 'I know it's going to come back,' she keeps saying. 'It's going to get me after all.' I can't find a way to make her feel better, no matter what I try. It's awful."

Such anxiety is so common it's been given an informal medical designation: the "Sword of Damocles Syndrome." Named for a mythological story in which a man lives in the shadow of a lethal sword that might fall on him at any time, it denotes the sense of ever-impending threat that some survivors feel in remission. The consequences of living with this long-term constant anxiety have been well-documented: high blood pressure, decreased appetite and strength, depression. Preliminary studies suggest that those who suffer this syndrome might actually be more likely to relapse.

Rather than engaging in a futile struggle against the inevitable, we would be wise to "befriend death" and school ourselves to think of it as a "gateway to new life," Henri Nouwen writes in *Our Greatest Gift: A Meditation on Dying and Caring.* Death is "the most human of all events," Nouwen insists, a communion of mortality that brings us into solidarity with each other and with the divine. Accepting that we must pass from our physical bodies signals acquiescence to God's will, a healthy and holy "surrender to the embrace of [the] Father."[4]

Nouwen's advice follows a long tradition of Christian thought that urges believers, as the Ash Wednesday admonition goes, always to "remember that you are dust, and to dust you shall return." This perspective was widely promulgated in medieval and early modern Europe, when life expectancy was short, sudden death was common, and the

Black Plague carried off about half the population. "Memento Mori," the concept was (and is) termed, "remember death." Works of art in multiple genres reminded people in that period of death's immanence. Portraits of healthy young people showed them holding skulls or posed with skeletons behind them. Shakespeare's Hamlet goes to a graveyard and addresses his jester's bones. Physician/philosopher Thomas Browne's seventeenth-century treatise *Hydriotaphia, Urn Burial*, reviews world funeral customs and meditates on death.

Such artistic expressions were understood not merely as providing morbid thrills but as serving a serious spiritual purpose. If people were reminded of their mortality, the thinking went, they were forced to acknowledge their dependence on God. They were also encouraged to prepare for death by living worthy lives in the present, lives of service, penance, and devotion. "Be careful of time," wrote St. Alphonsus Liguori a century after Browne, "which is the most precious thing and the greatest gift that God bestows upon living men." Every day, every single moment, he urged his readers, is an opportunity to grow in virtue, discipleship, and faith.[5]

Nor are such sentiments a feature of Christianity in particular, for the call to remember death and seize the day in a virtuous sense is near universal among world spiritual traditions. Buddhism pays it particular homage. Its followers were historically encouraged to meditate on death in situations that made it immediately, even horribly real: spending nights in graveyards, sitting up with corpses. Today meditative practices invite Buddhists to imagine their own deaths and the deaths of those they love. Such exercises, it is said, diffuse death's horror by bringing this primal fear into the light. They weaken our attachment to our egos, moving us toward wisdom. As it comes home to us that everyone will suffer and die, our compassion increases. "Life is a great teacher and death is a great teacher," writes Larry Rosenberg, a Buddhist writer and former psychology professor. "If we do open our hearts to this fact [of death] . . . it can be a great help to us. It can teach us how to live."[6]

Nobody needs less reminding of death's inevitability than professional hospice care workers, who wade into the river of mortality every morning. We live perennially with a kind of *memento mori* display before us. We may witness many passings; we will lose many whom we have come to love.

Yet those I've met who devote their lives to end-of-life care are not on the whole a morose and haunted group, but people able quietly and confidently to convey to those they serve the conviction that death is "perfectly safe" (to borrow an oft-repeated remark by Ram Das). It's common to hear them say that their faith has been deepened, even transformed by years of such work.

"It's so incredibly moving to witness a death," one hospice nurse affirmed. "Forty years ago when I started nursing I focused on obstetrics—I was so excited about bringing new life into the world. But as I got older myself it seemed natural to work with older people, and I discovered that being present at a death is a lot like helping with a birth. It feels like a transition, too." So often, she reported, she has felt an incredible, peaceful change. "I used to be kind of an agnostic about whether people had souls, whether there was more beyond this life, and so on. But not anymore. I'm convinced I've felt people's presences in the room after they've passed, and the pain and fear are gone. Something amazing has happened."

"It doesn't matter what religion you are or if you consider yourself 'spiritual' instead of religious, or even if you go in there not sure of what you think," another insisted. "Death is always sacred. Sure it can be hard, full of anxiety and suffering as it approaches. But once people are actually passing and just after, something changes and seems very beautiful, like people are going home."

I shivered as I listened, remembered one of my patients who had begun shortly after her ninety-eighth birthday to get up from her nursing home bed and wander. "I want to go home," she kept insisting.

She was just getting more confused, her granddaughter said, brushing off the new behavior. She'd forgotten that the facility was where she lived now, was confusing it with a hotel.

Three weeks later, however, the woman did go home in the sense referenced above.

My own education in befriending death began on the April evening in 2002 when my husband died. Though baptized Episcopalian, Ford had not been a religious man as an adult, unable to make peace with the abuses organized religion had visited on the world over so many centuries and with the hypocrisy of some religious leaders. He was always drawn to faith, however, with a palpable yearning. He loved literature that explored questions of life-beyond-life (William Wordsworth's "Prelude" and "Ode on Intimations of Immortality" were among his favorite poems). When one of his own compositions found its way into a volume entitled *Pacific Northwest Spiritual Poetry*, I started calling him "God's own agnostic." He favored the music of faith, both high (Bach's masses, the Mahler second symphony, the Berlioz Requiem) and low (the bluegrass gospel of his Virginia childhood). He read widely in theology, comparative religion, and the philosophy of religion.

Toward the end Ford became the person of surer faith in our home. It was my dying husband who insisted that I continue to attend Mass each Sunday; it was he who requested that I learn the rosary and pray it aloud as I sat beside him. He retrieved his grandfather's Book of Common Prayer and read it daily. He smiled up at the priest I'd called in to bless him.

By the final day Ford's sister and brother-in-law had come to help us, and the latter gave me one of the most precious gifts I've ever received. "Sit with him," he told me. "He can still hear." And so I spent the entire day beside Ford, the others coming and going, in that room with the curtain open to the mountain ridges outside gleaming with snow even as the first warm breeze of spring, the first birdsong, drifted into the room. I heard myself speak with absolute peace about our love, our marriage, asking forgiveness for the harms I had done him—the inevitable harms all married people know, and the harms specific to us. He nodded, murmured, reached toward my hand, Ford distilled to his gentlest self, the tensions of the previous weeks gone. That day we held a conversation that bridged several languages—speech and intonation and gesture—remembering the great and small joys of our life together, the places we loved, the ways we'd become one.

As the afternoon lengthened and my husband's breathing began to rasp, I heard myself reassure him that he should concentrate on the passage before him instead of worrying about me. Time would pass so quickly for him, my voice told him, that even if I lived as long as my grandmother, then an incredible 103, it would seem that I'd be beside him tomorrow. He nodded, said something calm and indistinguishable. I talked of dead friends, asking him to imagine dinner with them later that night—a climbing partner who had fallen to his death, a union organizer friend who'd died of brain cancer, his mother. I heard myself say these things with surety, and I believed them.

He lingered till his best friend came to join us, and we sat together in the bedroom as the twilight glow faded from the ridge. No wild pain, no cries, none of the hallucinations the doctors had warned might come. Just the mystery in the room, the wonder, and our quiet voices urging him to let go. Just breath slowing in longer intervals, then a pause, another breath, another pause, longer this time, until no breath came again. Then a great peace, a sense of being wrapped in love.

"So what do you think happens?" The woman leaned toward me, aggressive, the cake on her plate forgotten. *Why wouldn't she let this go? She was a guest at my table, for crying out loud.*

We'd both had one too many glasses of wine, I'll admit. I'd have been wise to refuse the bait when she began mocking Christianity (I'd known she was an evangelical atheist). Still, I'd been proud of myself for exercising restraint, for not going too far in defender-of-the-faith mode at this birthday party for a friend of mine whose friend she was. When asked the question direct I'd simply said that yes, I was a Catholic and, though I admitted that the church was far from perfect as a human institution, had found much to sustain and challenge me in its practice and doctrine.

Then I'd attempted to turn the conversation to another topic—had she heard that article on art conservation on NPR?

But she would not back off. "So, tell me what you believe about 'heaven,'" she sneered. "Robes? Harps? What age are the bodies?"

I'd always thought of such pictures of the afterlife as allegories, I told her. I didn't pretend to know. I simply trusted, imagining some kind of wonderful unity.

What? How could I say I was a Catholic if I didn't know what I thought about something so fundamental as heaven? That evening did not end well, as you might imagine.

Yet it did not make me imagine that pinning down exactly what I "know" about what comes next would be good or necessary. Even that paramount apostle St. Paul, after all, insists that as mere mortal beings we can understand the mysteries of faith only "through a glass, darkly" (that specific lovely phrase is from the King James translation), alluding to the polished metal mirrors for which Corinth was famous. "At present I know partially," he says of himself, but after death "I shall know fully, as I am fully known" (1 Cor 13:12).

It's absurd to pretend or presume that we are capable of describing (or even vaguely conceiving) details about what happens after death. We can still witness with our lives, though, that we trust that something marvelous and absolutely right does.

"As we learn, over time, to live the truth that death does not have a sting, we find within ourselves the gift to guide others to discover the same truth," Henri Nouwen writes. Hospice workers are in the perfect position to draw on that advice as we summon a respectful, attentive, and steadfastly poised affect that proclaims *there's nothing to fear* and *your spirit matters*. We can serve, in Nouwen's words, as "living reminder[s] that a person is indeed a beloved child of God," as we create "that place where our dying friends can feel safe and can gradually let go and make the passage knowing they are loved."[7]

If you've done much work with aging people, you'll almost certainly have been invited into conversations with them about the last things, a situation that poses distinctive challenges of how much to say, how sure to be.

"Where's my mama and daddy?" Cora asks, clear-eyed and insistent. One of my original and favorite patients, Cora has lingered in hospice for four years, declining slowly from dementia and a host of age-related issues. At age one hundred she's even more unstuck in time and place than when we initially met but still every bit as friendly and talkative. She still grabs and kisses my hand when efforts to relax her arthritically clawed ones succeed; she's still apt to say the darndest, most out-of-nowhere things.

"Where's my mama and daddy?" she repeats, regarding me with insistent urgency.

I don't believe in lying to the aged if something like the truth can be told with gentleness. I've witnessed the anguish Cora feels because the sad fact of her beloved elder sister's death is being purposefully withheld from her. Cora's descendants believe that learning the obvious will break her spirit, but sometimes Cora realizes that her sister doesn't telephone from Utah anymore and frets with obvious pain, imagining that she is somehow responsible for a rift. "I'm afraid Clara's mad at me, but I can't think what I did," she laments.

Her parents are a different matter, though, since Cora is at some level fully cognizant of the fact that they've been long gone. She's repeatedly told me about her father's sudden death from a heart attack in front of the whole family, about her mother's unrelenting labors to shepherd eight children to adulthood "and then she was just worn out and knew we'd be all right and went to be with Daddy."

So the truth will not be revelatory in an absolute sense. But how it's delivered matters.

I take a deep breath and look around Cora's room, registering again the big photograph of the Mormon temple in Salt Lake City. *Okay, then.*

"I think they're in heaven," I tell her, reassuringly squeezing the hand that grips mine.

Cora stares back at me, her mouth working. This cogitation goes on for ten or fifteen seconds, and I begin to fear that I've upset her.

Abruptly her face relaxes and she grins. "Well, that's a good place for them!" she crows.

Then that little bow mouth begins to work again.

"Do you think I'm goin' to heaven too?"

That one's easy. "Absolutely, Cora."

"And I'll see you there!"

"I hope so," I tell her.

At that an expression I've not seen before comes over her face, one that looks almost like embarrassment.

"A LONG time from now," Cora quickly qualifies. "You're young!"

Empathy is a rare capacity in dementia, but during this little conversation about faith it has just blossomed, bright and absolute.

From childhood I've loved the hymn "This Is My Father's World." As the title suggests, it celebrates the beauty of the created universe, along the way offering gratitude for human love in the form of "friends on earth and friends above."[8]

When I was a child inhabiting a safe and comfortable 1950s American middle-class youth—a life so charmed that no one I loved died until I was in my late twenties—that latter phrase always struck me as sweet and old-fashioned but abstract, like a sentimental deathbed scene in an old novel.

Now, of course, I know lots of dead people. I could light so many votive candles at Mass that the whole four-row rack is appropriated, but I don't, restraining myself each week to one for Ford along with a few for patients who have died recently and/or friends/family members gone to their rest. I like to fancy that doing so brings these spirits into each other's presence, wherever/whatever they are, encouraging them to get acquainted, maybe even to talk about me, at least for the duration of the wick's life. I whimsically arrange conversation groups, I'll admit, in the spirit of those "if you could ask any four people from history to dinner" games. Sometimes the people in line behind me get a little antsy—*is she going to leave any candles for us?*

They have nothing to worry about, however, for I'm careful always to leave plenty of candles for others, understanding how good it is for everyone to remember those who have gone before us. In a sense those candles aren't just for the dead ones' souls, but for ours too. Lighting them recalls love. It voices belief in continued connection. It expresses the hope that our prayers for them and their intercessions for us may have some share in bringing all of us into the Mystery's presence in reasonably good trim.

All that said, I am not fooling myself about the prospect of facing my own death with absolutely calm equanimity. As a person who, as noted earlier in this book, has long attempted to keep a tight grip on the wheel of her life's trajectory (and still admittedly prefers to steer), I anticipate difficulties with that final and absolute surrender. As someone who loves the created earth, I know that I'll resist abandoning those "rocks and trees, skies and seas" mentioned in that favorite hymn.

I hope, thus, that my transition might be smoothed by those people for whom I light those candles each week, that they will become in their turn "befrienders" for me. I anticipate that I'm going to need those sweet souls to help midwife me over the threshold, calmly reassuring me with *your spirit matters* during the hardest parts.

And once that passage is over, I hope to join them in celebrating a glorious new reality where dying, to borrow a phrase from the poet Walt Whitman's "Song of Myself," is revealed as "different from what anyone supposed, and luckier." [9]

Afterword: Many Parts

While working on this book in the summer of 2018 I took a break to travel across the country to see my ninety-three-year-old mother and her husband in Philadelphia. The visit promised to be a relatively low-stress affair, since the two of them had recently moved into an apartment in an assisted-living facility, a much better circumstance for them (and for visitors, I admit to relief about) than previously. My mother was considerably more alert and happier than she had been in the little house where they'd lived for decades, with its single bathroom up a flight of stairs, increasingly cluttered conditions, uncertain nutrition, and increased isolation as her mobility had declined. In the comfortable, nay exemplary, facility she'd gained friends who lived just down the hall, fresh subjects for conversation, and a sunny and open one-floor apartment in a wing of the place that was brand new. There would be a separate guest lodging for me a quarter mile away, promising privacy and quiet space to read in the early mornings.

In the weeks leading up to that trip, however, I woke in the night with apprehension about transportation logistics. The plan was for me to fly in from Idaho not to Philadelphia but to Washington, DC, combining the filial visit with a conference to follow in the latter city. I'd reserved a rental car for the inter-city round-trip commute rather than buying

Amtrak tickets since no one was available to retrieve me from the suburban commuter-train station where I'd be deposited and I knew I'd want independent mobility during the days with my mother.

This arrangement seemed very reasonable four months ahead. As the date approached, though, I couldn't stop picturing that three-hundred-mile commute through the gut of the East Coast interstate corridor. I'm a reasonably brave and very experienced driver, but the prospect of solo negotiation of I-95 and its multiple city bypasses proved definitely intimidating.

In actuality, however, the most perilous driving environment I encountered on that trip was not the Washington, DC, Inner Loop, nor I-95 itself, nor the Baltimore Beltway, nor the congested Blue Route west of Philadelphia, nor the Pennsylvania Turnpike. It was the nearly empty parking lot of the facility where my mother now resides. Peril manifested on the visit's second night, as I was backing up after a full day of two-on-one agreeableness and patience. More-than-ready for the silence of the guest house, weary in my bones, I don't think I glanced in the rear-view mirror as I threw the car into reverse. Instead I sensed rather than saw or heard something and abruptly slammed on the brakes. Another woman glazed from a day with her aged relative(s) and I had come within inches of colliding as she, too, backed up without looking.

In the vicinity of Philadelphia such a situation might inspire—even between middle-aged women—outraged blasts of the horn, perhaps a barrage of shouted rude comments and/or even an exchange of fingers. In that moment, however, we simply smiled and shrugged as our eyes met. I pulled back into the space to give her room and she turned toward the highway with a wave.

That little incident, with its reminder of community and its call to mercy for self and others, cheered and comforted me in just the way I needed to be cheered and comforted that night. When I recounted it in the following days to others who were caring or had cared for people nearing life's end, it inspired gentle smiles. *That's the way it is, all right*, their nods or outright words said. *I've been there.*

I've been a member of many groups over the past seven decades—English professors, writers, Catholics, public humanists, critical thinkers, knitters, mountaineers, widows, massage therapists, etc. This fellowship of "caregivers," however, might be the tightest one of all.

For accepting the vocation of caregiver means becoming an initiate into arcane matters. As this book has tried to suggest, taking on this work entails not only gaining new expertise but also opening to fundamental, often difficult questions about the human condition. Those who care for the elderly and the dying regularly encounter existential quandaries about life and death and faith— quandaries that many outside our fraternity shrink from facing. We necessarily encounter the Mystery, living as we do in its shadow.

The nature of the work means also that all such ministers will also sooner or later be invited to undertake challenging self-examination. Working with the suffering and the dying has a way of bringing out weaknesses and fears, venial self-protective tendencies, and character flaws. Caregivers will inevitably be brought—perhaps as few other occupational groups are—to acknowledge their common membership in the imperfect, sinning human race.

Yet such practice also promises insight guaranteed to gladden hearts and lift spirits. Those who persist with faith in the vocation of caring for the elderly and the dying, who open to learning and to inspiration, will encounter inevitably in themselves and in others the most marvelous innate human capacities, including talents for selflessness, for tolerance and forgiveness, for courage, and for trust, and they'll discover that those capacities will expand with use. Caregivers are uniquely placed to witness the love both human and divine that always folds us in, even when we feel most alone, and such witnessing holds the power to transform our lives through holy surrender, to infuse them with joyful hope.

May you find deep satisfaction in this work and be a blessing to all you serve, sustained by the Mystery's love and care. May this ministry prove ultimately life-giving for you, as it has been for me.

Pocatello, Idaho
December 4, 2018

Notes

Introduction

    1. Joan Chittister, *The Gift of Years: Growing Older Gracefully* (New York: BlueBridge, 2008), xv.

    2. D'Vera Cohn and Paul Taylor, "Baby Boomers Approach 65—Glumly," Pew Research Center, December 20, 2010, www.pewsocialtrends.org/2010/12/20/baby-boomers-approach-65-glumly/.

    3. Avery Comarow et al., "Nursing Home Finder," *US News and World Report*, November 2016, https://www.usnews.com/static/documents/health/nursing-homes/BNH_2016-17_Methodology.pdf.

    4. For a history of the hospice movement, see Stephen P. Kiernan, *Last Rights: Rescuing the End of Life from the Medical System* (New York: MacMillan, 2007).

    5. "Caregiving in the US," AARP, June 15, 2015, https://www.aarp.org/content/dam/aarp/ppi/2015/caregiving-in-the-united-states-2015-report-revised.pdf.

    6. An excellent array of statistics on geriatric healthcare appears in *Retooling for an Aging America: Building the Health Care Workforce*, Institute of Medicine (US) Committee on the Future Health Care Workforce for Older Americans (Washington, DC: National Academies Press, 2008).

    7. "NHPCO's Facts and Figures: Hospice Care in America," National Hospice and Palliative Care Organization, 2014, cited in Rachel Burbeck et al., "Volunteers in Specialist Palliative Care: A Survey of Adult Services in the United Kingdom," *Journal of Palliative Medicine* 17, no. 5 (May 2014): 568–74.

8. See, for example, Rohr's *Falling Upward: A Spirituality for the Two Halves of Life* (San Francisco: Jossey-Bass, 2011).

9. *Apostolicum Actuositatem*, promulgated by Pope Paul VI, November 18, 1965.

10. *First Rule of the Friars Minor*, 17 ("Of Preachers").

11. US Conference of Catholic Bishops, "Blessings of Age Text: A Pastoral Message in Growing Older With the Faith Community," 1999.

Chapter 1

1. Thomas Merton, *No Man Is an Island* (New York: Harcourt Brace, 1955), 131, 133.

2. Quoted in Boniface Hanley, *With Minds of Their Own: Eight Women Who Made a Difference* (Notre Dame, IN: Ave Maria Press, 1991), 89.

3. Pseudo-John Chrysostom, "On the Annunciation of the Blessed Virgin," homily (fourth century).

4. Jean-Pierre de Caussade, *Abandonment to Divine Providence*, 1861.

5. David Richo, *Mary Within: A Jungian Contemplation of Her Titles and Powers* (New York: The Crossroad Publishing Company, 2001), 44.

6. Merton, *No Man Is An Island*, 140–41.

Chapter 2

1. *The Poetry of Robert Frost: The Collected Poems, Complete and Unabridged* (New York: Holt, Rinehart, and Winston, 1969), 119.

2. For a discussion of America's devaluation of the elderly, see William H. Thomas, *What Are Old People For? How Elders Will Save the World* (Acton, MA: Vanderwyk, 2004). Representative among alarmist commentary is Eric Schnurer, "Baby Boomers Are Ruining the Budget for Everyone," *US News and World Report*, October 16, 2013, https://www.usnews.com/opinion/blogs/eric-schnurer/2013/10/16/baby-boomers-are-running-up-the-national-debt-and-undermining-education.

3. Quoted in Carolyn Gregoire, "How Changing the Way You Think About Death Can Transform the Way You Live," *Huffington Post*, August 30, 2013, https://www.huffingtonpost.com.au /entry/how-changing-the-way-you-_n_3790274.html.

4. See, in this context, chapter 4 ("Tragedy") in *What Are Old People For?*

5. Gabriel Sahlgren, "Work Longer, Live Healthier: The relationship between economic activity, health, and government policy," Age Endeavour Fellowship and Institute for Economic Affairs, 2013, http://www.cardi.ie/publications/worklongerlivehealthierthe relationshipbetweeneconomicactivityhealthandgovernmentpolicy.

6. Amy Fiske et al., "Depression in Older Adults," *Annual Review of Clinical Psychology*, no. 5 (April 27, 2009): 363–89.

7. Atul Gawande, *Being Mortal: Medicine and What Matters in the End* (New York: Picador, 2014), 141.

8. An excellent introduction to the subject is Stephen M. Marson and Rasby M. Powell's "Goffman and the Infantilization of Elderly Persons: A Theory of Development," *The Journal of Sociology and Social Work* 41, no. 4 (December 2014): 142–58.

9. Pope Francis, "The Family, 6. The Elderly," General Address, St. Peter's Square, March 4, 2015.

10. USCCB, "Blessings of Age Text."

11. Lewis Richmond, *Aging as a Spiritual Practice: A Contemplative Guide to Growing Older and Wiser* (New York: Penguin, 2012).

12. Thomas Moore, *Ageless Soul: The Lifelong Journey Toward Meaning and Joy* (New York: St. Martin's, 2017).

13. Chittister, *The Gift of Years*, 25, x, xi.

14. Rohr, *Falling Upward*, 157.

15. Rohr, *Falling Upward*, 124.

Chapter 3

1. Paul Ingraham, "Massage Therapy, Does It Work? A Review of the Science of Massage Therapy . . . Such as It Is," Pain Science, July 18, 2018, https://www.painscience.com/articles/does-massage -work.php.

2. For a review of research on the effects of touch, see Tiffany Field, *Massage Therapy Research* (London: Churchill Livingstone, 2006).

3. Gayle MacDonald, "Massage as a Respite Intervention for Primary Caregivers," *The Journal of Hospice and Palliative Care* 15, no. 1 (January 1998): 43–47.

4. See Jeanette Templin, "Music Therapy for Adults with Traumatic Brain Injury or Other Neurological Disorders," in *Music Therapy Handbook*, ed. Barbara Wheeler (Guilford Press, 2017), 454–67; Clare O'Callaghan et al., "Music Therapy at the End of Life," in *Music Therapy Handbook*, 468–80; and Andrew Schulman's first-hand account of providing music therapy, *Waking the Spirit: A Musician's Journey to Healing Body, Mind, and Spirit* (New York: Picador, 2016).

5. For a biography, see Kathryn Spink, *Mother Teresa: An Authorized Biography* (New York: HarperOne, 2011); for a compilation of Teresa's sayings, see Carol Kelly-Gang's *Mother Teresa: Quotable Wisdom* (Asheville, NC: Fall River Press, 2014).

6. Kyu-taik Sung and Ruth E. Dunkle, "How Social Workers Demonstrate Respect for Elderly Clients," *Journal of Gerontological Social Work* 52, no. 3 (April 2009): 250–60.

Chapter 4

1. Mario Garrett, "Incidence—and Fear—of Dementia Increase with Life Expectancy," *The San Diego Union-Tribune*, July 19, 2011, www.sandiegotribune.com/sdut-incidence-and-fear-of -dementia-increase-with-life-2011jul19-story.html.

2. Stephen G. Post, *The Moral Challenge of Alzheimer Disease: Ethical Issues from Diagnosis to Dying* (Baltimore: Johns Hopkins Press, 2000).

3. Good sources of information on dementia are the websites of the Dementia Society of America (http://www.dementiasociety .org) and the Alzheimer's Association (https://www.alz.org/).

4. Perla Werner, "Family Stigma and Caregiver Burden in Alzheimer's Disease," *The Gerontologist* 52, no. 1 (February 2012): 80–97.

5. Rabbi Cary Kozberg, "A Jewish Response to Dementia: Honoring Broken Tablets," http://www.caregiverslibrary.org/portals/0/Microsoft%20Word%20-%20A%20Jewish%20Response%20to%20Dementia[1].pdf.

6. Thrangu Rinpoche is quoted in Lewis Richmond, "Fear of Dementia," March 4, 2011, https://www.loinsroar.com/fear-of-dementia-a-guest-post-by-lewis-richmond/.

7. Pope John Paul II, *Evangelium Vitae*, promulgated March 25, 1995.

8. For a compilation of information on dementia research as well as philosophical essays on the subject of memory disorder, see the multivolume set *Aging, Spiritual, and Religion: A Handbook*, ed. Melvin A. Kimble and Susan H. McFadden (Minneapolis: Fortress Press, 1995, 2003).

Chapter 5

1. For a discussion of humor's effects, see "Philosophy of Humor," in *The Stanford Encyclopedia of Humor* (2012, rev. 2016), https://plato.stanford.edu/entries/humor. See also Victor Raskin, *The Primer of Humor Research* (Berlin: DeGruyter, 2009).

2. See, for instance, Martha Buffum, "Humor and Well-Being in Spouse Caregivers of Patients with Alzheimer's Disease," *Applied Nursing* 11, no. 1 (February 1998): 12–18; and L. F. Law et al., "The Effects of Humor Therapy on Nursing Home Residents Measured Using Observational Methods: The SMILE Cluster Randomized Trial," *Journal of the Medical Directors Association* 15, no. 8 (August 2014): 564–69.

3. "Philosophy of Humor."

4. James Martin, *Between Heaven and Mirth: Why Joy, Humor, and Laughter Are at the Heart of the Spiritual Life* (New York: HarperCollins, 2001), 88–92, 194–206.

5. Martin, *Between Heaven and Mirth*, 95, 115–17.

6. See susansparks.com.

Chapter 6

1. Arif H. Kamal et al., "Prevalence and Predictors of Burnout among Hospice and Palliative Care Clinicians in the US," *Journal*

of Pain Symptom Management 51, no. 14 (April 2016): 690–98; Vicki Rackner, "Eight Tips to Managing Caregiver Guilt," *Today's Caregiver*, https://caregiver.com/articles/managing_caregiver _guilt/.

2. Susan C. Reinhard et al., "Supporting Family Caregivers in Providing Care," in *Patient Safety and Quality: An Evidence-Based Handbook for Nurses*, ed. R. G. Hughes (Rockville, MD: Agency for Healthcare Research and Quality, 2008); Cristina Dobre et al., "Efficient Measures for Burnout in Palliative Care," *International Journal of Medical Dentistry* 21, no. 2 (April–June 2017): 81–84.

3. "Caregiver Stress: Tips for Taking Care of Yourself," Mayo Clinic, https://www.mayoclinic.org/healthy-lifestyle/stress-manage ment/in-depth/caregiver-stress-art-20044784.

4. Kamal et al., "Prevalence and Predictors."

5. Dio Kavalieratos et al., "'It's Like Heart Failure. It's Chronic . . . and It Will Kill You': A Qualitative Analysis of Burnout," *Journal of Pain Symptom Management* 53, no. 5 (May 2017): 901–10.

6. Catherin Ward-Griffin and Patricia McKeever, "Relationships Between Nurses and Family Caregivers: Partners in Care?," *Advances in Nursing Science* 22, no. 3 (March 2000): 89–103.

7. Statistics come from the Gallup-Hathaway Well-Being Index, 2011, cited in Dan Witters, "The Cost of Caregiving to the U.S. Economy," *Business Journal*, December 1, 2011, https://news.gallup .com/businessjournal/151049/cost-caregiving-economy.aspx.

8. Emily Harrop et al., "'It Still Haunts Me Whether We Did the Right Thing:' A Qualitative Analysis of Free Text Survey Data in the Bereavement Experiences and Support Needs of Family Caregivers," *BioMed Central Palliative Care*, no. 15 (October 2016): 92–100. See also the website of the Center for Complicated Grief, http://complicatedgrief.columbia.edu.

9. J. R. Day et al., "Compassion Fatigue in Adult Daughter Caregivers of a Parent with Dementia," *Issues in Mental Health Nursing* 35, no. 10 (October 2015): 796–804.

Chapter 7

1. A representative set of such hints is Karen Brooks, "Violence in the Field: 37 Safety Tips for Home Healthcare Providers," Kinser Software Home Health Blog, April 11, 2012, https://kinnser.com/home-health-blog/post/violence-in-the-field-37-safety-tips-for-home-healthcare-providers/.

Chapter 8

1. St. Gregory of Nazianzus, Oration 41, On Pentecost (fourth century), parts 6 and 7.

2. Text: 77 77 D; fr. the Pentecost Sequence, *Veni, Sancte Spiritus*, alt.; adapt. by Owen Alstott, b. 1947, © 1980, OCP. All rights reserved. Used with permission.

Chapter 9

1. Charles Austin Miles, "In the Garden," 1913.

2. For a brief introduction to energy work, see https://www.shape.com/lifestyle/mind-and-body/what-is-energy-work. Individual modalities have their own professional organizations and informational websites, searchable by keyword.

3. At least eighty nursing schools teach energy work, most often Therapeutic Touch; among the hospitals open to some energy modalities are Mt. Sinai and George Washington University.

4. US Conference of Catholic Bishops, Committee on Doctrine, "Guidelines for Evaluating Reiki as an Alternate Therapy," March 25, 2009.

5. The allusion is to Matthew 7:15-20.

6. Alfred, Lord Tennyson, "In Memoriam A. H. H.," 1850.

Chapter 10

1. See, for example, Stephen Jenkinson's impassioned treatise, *Die Wise: A Manual for Sanity and Soul* (Berkeley, CA: North Atlantic Books, 2015).

2. Gawande, *Being Mortal*.

3. Zalman Schachter-Shalomi and Ronald S. Miller, *From Age-ing to Sage-ing: A Profound New Vision of Growing Older* (New York: Warner Books, 1995), 90.

4. Henri Nouwen, *Our Greatest Gift: A Meditation on Dying and Caring* (New York: HarperCollins, 1985), 47, 79, 61.

5. St. Alphonsus Liguori, *Preparation for Death: Considerations On Eternal Truth*, 1868.

6. Larry Rosenberg, "The Third Messenger: Death is Unavoidable," in *Awake at the Bedside: Contemplative Teachings in Palliative and End-of-Life Care*, ed. K. P. Ellison (Somerville, MA: Wisdom Publications, 2016), 215–34.

7. Nouwen, *Our Greatest Gift*, 61, 63.

8. Maltbie D. Babcock, "This Is My Father's World," 1901.

9. Walt Whitman, "Song of Myself," *Leaves of Grass*, 1892.

Further Readings

Brchony, Kathleen A. *After the Darkest Hour: How Suffering Begins the Journey to Wisdom.* New York: Henry Holt, 2000.

Brock, Ira. *Dying Well: Peace and Possibilities at the End of Life.* New York: The Berkeley Publishing Group, 1997.

Chittister, Joan. *The Gift of Years: Growing Older Gracefully.* New York: BlueBridge, 2008.

Dunlop, John. *Finding Grace in the Face of Dementia.* Wheaton, IL: Crossway, 2017.

Ellison, Koshin Pale, and Matt Weingast, eds. *Awake at the Bedside: Contemplative Teachings on Palliative and End-of-Life Care.* Somerville, MA: Wisdom Publications, 2016.

Gawande, Atul. *Being Mortal: Medicine and What Matters at the End.* New York: Picador, 2014.

Kiernan, Stephen P. *Last Rites: Rescuing the End of Life From the Medical System.* New York: MacMillan, 2007.

Kimbel, Melvin, and Susan McFadden, eds. *Aging, Spirituality, and Religion: A Handbook.* 2 vols. Minneapolis: Augsburg Fortress Press, 1995, 2003.

Martin, James. *Between Heaven and Mirth: Why Joy, Humor, and Laughter Are at the Heart of the Spiritual Life.* New York: HarperCollins, 2011.

Moore, Thomas. *Ageless Soul: The Lifelong Journey Toward Meaning and Joy.* New York: St. Martin's, 2017.

Nouwen, Henri. *Our Greatest Gift: A Meditation on Dying and Caring.* New York: HarperCollins, 1985.

Ram Das, and Mirabai Bush. *Walking Each Other Home: Conversations on Loving and Dying.* Sounds True, 2018.

Richmond, Lewis. *Aging as a Spiritual Practice: A Contemplative Guide to Growing Older and Wiser.* New York: Penguin, 2012.

Rohr, Richard. *Falling Upward: A Spirituality for the Two Halves of Life.* San Francisco: Jossey-Bass, 2011.

Schacter-Shalomi, Zalman, and Ronald S. Miller. *From Age-ing to Sage-ing: A Profound New Vision of Getting Older.* New York: Warner Books, 1995.

Schmidt, Mark A. *Into Your Hands Lord: A Catholic Companion to Dying and Hospice Care.* 2013. www.createspace.com/4184632.

Schulman, Andrew. *Waking the Spirit: A Musician's Journey to Healing Body, Mind, and Soul.* New York: Picador, 2016.

Strada, E. Alessandra. *The Helping Professional's Guide to End-of-Life Care: Practical Tools for Emotion, Social and Spiritual Support for the Dying.* Oakland, CA: New Harbinger Publications, 2013.

Thomas, William H. *What Are Old People For? How Elders Will Save the World.* Action, MA: Vanderwyk and Burnham, 2004.

Yoder, Greg. *Companioning the Dying: A Soulful Guide for Caregivers.* Ft. Collins, CO: Companion Press, 2005.